PLAY A PART

PLAY A PART

Bernice Wells Carlson

Drawings by Catherine H. Scholz

Nashville ABINGDON PRESS *New York*

Printed in the United States of America

ISBN 0-687-31637-5
Library of Congress Catalog Card Number: 72-95198

To
my grandchildren
Robert, Nancy, and David Umberger

BOOKS by BERNICE WELLS CARLSON

Act It Out

Do It Yourself—Tricks, Stunts, and Skits

Fun for One—or Two

The Junior Party Book

Listen! And Help Tell the Story

Make It and Use It

Make It Yourself

The Party Book for Boys and Girls

Play a Part

The Right Play for You

You Know What? I Like Animals

BERNICE WELLS CARLSON

with David R. Ginglend

Play Activities for the Retarded Child

Recreation for Retarded Teenagers and Young Adults

BERNICE WELLS CARLSON

with Kari Hunt

Masks and Mask Makers

ACKNOWLEDGMENTS

I should like to thank the many boys and girls who helped me prepare this book over a period of years—children in public schools, in church-related programs, in summer recreation activities, at residential camps, Cub Scouts, Brownies, and Girl Scouts, the children of my own neighborhood, and most of all my own two children, Christine and Philip, who when in a play always played a part from start to finish, regardless of the size of the role.

I should like also to thank a number of people who offered professional help, especially Mrs. D. S. Wilt, teacher, Cranford, New Jersey Public Schools; Mary Ellen Lindley, formerly coordinator of children's services, Maui Public Library, Hawaii; Mrs. Joyce Haas, doctoral student, Rutgers University Library School; Mrs. Lloyd Smith, librarian, Franklin Township, New Jersey; and Mrs. Robert Barnett, program specialist, Girl Scouts, U.S.A.

—Bernice Wells Carlson

CONTENTS

YOU, THE PLAY, AND THE PLAYERS

Every Inch an Actor

Almost everyone wishes at times that for a little while at least he might become some other person—or a bird, or an imaginary creature, or some animal. A play, a skit, or a puppet show may give you the perfect opportunity to be for a few minutes, or for even an hour, an ancient pharaoh counseling his people, Cleopatra floating down the Nile River, a red-nosed reindeer, Queen Victoria, Charles Lindbergh, a dolphin splashing through the sea, or Neil Armstrong saying, "Eagle has landed."

It isn't always easy, this being someone else, but it can be great fun. When you are an actor or an actress in any kind of production, play your part every moment you are onstage. Try to feel like the person or animal you are portraying. Act and speak like him. Stay in character all the time. Be every inch an actor.

In order to play a part well you must first of all understand the play. In every play there is a struggle, not necessarily a fight or other physical struggle, but a problem caused by people or groups of people with different ideas; or a problem caused by an event that affects the lives of many people—a war or a natural disaster, such as a flood; or some other kind of problem. As you read the play in which you are interested, ask yourself "What is the struggle in this play?"

In a fairy story, for example, a prince wants to marry a certain princess. He soon learns that a number of other princes also want to marry this same princess. Here is a struggle of princes, each wanting to prove that he is the most fit to marry the princess and each with his own idea of fitness; the strongest, or richest, or wisest, or most handsome, or most fun, or, in some cases, the kindest.

If you are chosen to be a prince, ask, "How does a prince act?" Traditionally a prince is dignified, stands up straight, speaks politely. A prince on stage should never slouch or answer, "Yah," or "Yep." An actor portraying a prince must be every inch a prince every minute he is onstage. But that is not enough.

You are going to play the part of a particular prince, not just any prince. You must ask, "What is the role of *my* prince?"

If your prince wishes to prove that he is the strongest, he may walk and talk like Superman. If he wishes to prove that he is the richest, he will exhibit his wealth. He may wave his jeweled hands in the air as he talks and extend his arms to display his expensive robes.

If your prince wants to prove that he is the kindest, what then? You must study a person you consider to be especially kind. See if his tone of voice has a special quality. Notice how he listens. Is he intent on what you are saying, or is he impatient to take over the conversation and talk about himself? Study other people you consider to be kind. Observe what qualities they seem to have—the things that make them kind.

As you study kind people, ask yourself, "Why is this person kind to me and to other people?" Then, getting back to your prince in your play, ask, "Why is my prince kind when others are not? Why does he want to marry this special princess? How does he feel about the kingdom and the people in it? How does he feel about other characters in this play?"

As you study the role of your prince in the play you will develop two abilities that are important to every good actor and actress: 1) the ability to observe and then act like some other person; 2) the ability to understand other people and thus to feel like another person. A good actor develops *sight* and *insight.*

In most plays, no one character acts alone. Other people enter the struggle which makes up the plot or story. You must, therefore, ask "What is the role of each character in the play? How does my prince act toward these other characters? And what is their reaction to him?"

A successful play represents teamwork. When one actor goes

beyond his role and tries to be more important than the author of the play intended him to be, he is no longer in character.

What about the minor roles in a play? "All right," someone may say, "so the actor playing the prince needs sight and insight. But I'm just a guard in the palace. All I say is 'Enter. The royal family awaits your coming.' Do I need sight and insight for my part?"

The answer comes quickly: "You do, indeed, Guard. A minor character needs sight and insight. Tell me, Guard, what is your role?"

"To guard the royal family, I suppose, just in case something happens."

"How will you stand while guarding the royal family?"

"Straight."

"All the time?"

"Yes, all the time."

"All right, Guard, you are standing straight and motionless. What about your eyes?"

"I'm watching carefully, just in case something unexpected happens."

"You're watching all the time?"

"Yes. All the time."

"Right you are, Guard. Remember, too, that a guard's manner must show that he is a person of dignity, due the greatest respect. Not everybody is entrusted with guarding the royal family. Guards that announce the arrival of a prince in an impressive way and then slouch, fidget, or giggle, or let their attention wander are poor guards and poor actors.

In order to understand the importance of minor characters who must feel their parts and play them from start to finish, let's look at two dramatic productions that were presented on the same day.

The TV screen showed a popular entertainer seated in an armchair with two boys and two girls seated on the floor near him.

As he told the Christmas story, quietly and simply, the children listened with wide-eyed wonderment. These children had no speaking parts and they were not moving about, but the expressions on their faces told the audience that they felt they were listening to a most wonderful story.

PLAY A PART

Were these children acting? Without saying a word? Without moving about? Indeed, they were acting. Each was playing the part of a boy or girl who loved to hear again the old, old story of the night when Jesus Christ was born. Not one let his attention wander. Each child understood his own role and stayed in character every minute.

Earlier that same day some kindergarten children had enacted the Nativity scene at a village church. As the choir told the story in song, Mary, Joseph, shepherds, wise men, and little angels gazed in mystic wonderment at the lighted manger. It was an inspiring scene until one angel, Betsy Greene, waved to her parents in the audience. The spell was broken. Betsy was no longer an angel. She was a bothersome child who did not feel her part, and had spoiled the mood of the whole play.

Do not be overly harsh in judging Betsy and all the other little angels who wave to parents from manger scenes each year. It takes time and imagination to become "a heavenly vision." It takes practice to appear to "float" rather than walk across a stage

like a child going to school. It takes insight to catch a sense of wonderment and then portray it. If Betsy has a part in a number of Christmas pageants she may become an angel—if she puts her mind and soul into a production.

No one becomes an outstanding actor overnight. Both time and practice are needed to develop the ability to observe people and act like them. It takes much thought to understand how people feel in certain situations and then to portray the feeling.

It takes time and practice to develop stage techniques. But many beginning actors are very good actors for three simple reasons: they feel their parts; they work well with other actors and with the director; and they stay in character.

So if you would like to be an actor, go right ahead. Choose a play. Get a group of friends together. Work together on rehearsals. Then when the production is ready and the time for the performance arrives, stay in character every moment you are onstage. Have fun being someone else for a little while. Really *play a part.*

The Right Play Right Now

In order to become an actor or actress, a person must advance from simple dramatics to more complicated interpretations. If you feel that you did not get an early start, don't worry. Choose something you feel you can do, and find an audience that will appreciate your efforts.

Girl Scouts who have had little opportunity to work together might choose as a starter not a full-length play but a puppet play, and present it before a Brownie audience. However, a puppet play is not the exclusive property of beginning actors. Experienced seventh graders might choose the same puppet play that the Girl Scouts chose, not because it is easy, but because the seventh graders feel that a certain group of kindergarten children would enjoy seeing it. A den of Cub Scouts might choose that same puppet play and perform it at a pack meeting.

Your own acting ability and the type of audience are only two factors you must consider in choosing a play. You must also think about your stage and type of equipment. Don't let either costumes or stage setting prevent you from doing a play with parts you really want to play. Costumes and stage settings do add atmosphere. But just as "clothes don't make the man," costumes do not make an actor, and a stage setting does not create a scene.

Costuming is a matter of local choice. Some groups may choose to perform plays in the kind of clothes they wear every day. Other groups may wish to make costumes out of any available material. Other groups may wish to appoint a committee to enlist the help of adults in making or getting authentic costumes. If you do use costumes, get them as soon as possible. Practice wearing them until they seem to be part of your role. If you play the part of a queen, walk like a queen and talk like a queen because you feel like a queen accustomed to wearing regal robes.

A "stage" may be an open spot near a campfire, or the front

of a classroom, or a professional stage. Settings may range from a plain stage with a few classroom chairs (and signs to indicate "trees" or "fountain" or whatever) to period furniture and an authentic backdrop. If you plan to use authentic scenery and props, try to have them as soon as possible after you begin rehearsals. Then, when you say your lines, you really can open a door or rise from a certain type of chair or do any other stage business that requires timing.

The material in this book is arranged to help you progress as an actor. Plays at the beginning of the book require less dramatic ability than those at the end.

Before you start to work on a play, read the introduction to that section, i.e., "Puppet Plays," "Skits," etc., and read also the introduction to the play itself. This will help you understand what you may learn as an actor from this particular experience. The introductions will help you understand also the play as a whole and help you to interpret the characters in the play.

Puppet Plays give players a chance to act together as a group without being self-conscious about facing an audience. Actors develop their voices and learn to use them effectively. They learn to listen and to come in on cue.

Skits allow an actor to "throw himself" into a part. The characters in skits are types of people who act and react with exaggerated zest.

In *Playlets and Dramatic Scenes* characters become real people for a short period. In these a character has less chance to develop than he might in a full-length play, but he does react sincerely as an individual to a given situation or to the opinions of other characters in the play.

The *Real-Life Drama* section, based on recorded events, is a combination of skits, dramatic scenes, and playlets. Actors are encouraged to study a historic period, and, in most cases, to read all they can about certain historic personages. They must then put themselves back in time to the date of the incident or event involved, and, finally, into the shoes of persons, real or imaginary, who are being portrayed.

Each of the *Plays* of the final section has an introduction, a middle, and a climax. Every actor is required to create a role and to take his character through a series of events. Regardless of the size of his roll, the actor must feel a part and play a part from start to finish.

What Are Your Lines?

What do you say? When do you say it? How do you say it? When you are acting, the lines—the spoken words—of a play must become a part of you. They must express to the audience the thoughts and ideas of the character you are portraying. They must let the audience know the kind of person you are portraying.

The lines of the play not only describe the characters, but also tell the story. You must first determine the purpose of each line of a play and then, if it is your line, decide how to say it; or, if it is the line of another actor, decide how you are going to react to it.

As you read a play pick out the key lines, the most important lines. These must be emphasized if the audience is to follow the plot of the play and understand a joke or a message. Of course every line of a play should be heard by the audience, but if your role contains certain key lines, plan to emphasize them.

There are several ways to emphasize key lines: (1) Exaggerate your manner of speaking. (2) Pause slightly before the key line if it follows something else you have said. This pause will cause other actors and the audience to focus full attention on you, and will give you an opportunity to take a deep breath that will enable you to say the line forcefully. (3) If someone else has the speech just before your key line, then before you say the line, call attention to yourself in some manner—turn abruptly or make some meaningful gesture.

Express key lines not only with your voice, but with your eyes and your body as well. Start to use this expression of feeling as you learn your lines and as you practice them, even when you are alone.

Remember, all the key lines are not yours. As part of a team you must help other actors put across their key lines. Look intently at a speaker and react to what he has said. Or, if the action or intent of the play suggests that you not be looking at the speaker, wait until he has finished, then look up and react or make some gesture that will indicate what your reaction is.

Suppose, for example, a mother in colonial America is sewing as she listens to her son tell of his efforts to teach a young slave. He says, "When Henry has learned a trade, and has learned to read, he shall be free." The mother drops her sewing in her lap and stares at her teen-aged son with an expression that seems to say, "I can't believe my ears."

The boy continues: "Henry shall be free. If this family will not free him when he is ready to earn a living, I shall work half my life to buy him—and then he shall be free." Whether the family decides to free the slave, or decides to let the son work half his life to free him, might form the plot of the play. But both the speaker and the silent actor helped to put across to the audience the key lines.

Information lines and filler lines in a play are not often dramatic, but they are vital because they help to set the scene and identify the special qualities of the characters. Some of these lines may appear at the beginning of a play. A few minutes after the rise of the curtain the audience must be able to identify the players who have appeared. A specific word that helps them do so may have much more importance than it would have at another time or place.

Suppose in the opening line of a play a girl named Janet says, "Come here, Tom," and Tom replies, "Just a moment, Sis." *Sis* is important here because it helps establish the relationship of Janet and Tom.

Important lines and filler lines often appear in the same scene. Suppose someone appears at a door, and Ma says in surprise, "Mr. Browning!" The audience gets Mr. Browning's name and the idea that he is someone of importance. When Ma continues, "Mr. Browning, these are my children. Children, this is Mr. Browning, president of the New Home Company," the audience knows who Mr. Browning is. Ma then introduces the children quickly, as handshakes take place, but there is no special emphasis on any word or line. These are filler lines which give more atmosphere than information.

As you study your part, examine short expressions that stand alone, such as "Never," "All right," or "I can't go." The tone of voice you use in saying them may tell the audience a lot more than the words themselves.

Take, for example, the words "all right." If a Scoutmaster tells you that you are to be in charge of setting up tents on a camping trip, you say "All right" with the meaning, "I understand. I'll do it."

If your mother tells you that you must go to a family gathering that you would like to skip, you say "All right" with the meaning, "I'm trapped. I'll go."

If a detective tells you he knows how to catch a thief but must depend on you to help, you answer, "All right" meaning "Let's go."

A *cue* is a speech or action in a play that serves as a signal for another actor to speak or act. Often you will be that actor, the one receiving the signal to speak or act. You must know and understand a play so well that your reaction to a cue comes as naturally as your reaction to an everyday conversation or situation. To make this possible you should learn an entire cue, not just the last few words. Then, if the other actor should change his speech even slightly, you can say your lines or act your part without holding up the production waiting for a specific word that never comes.

To *ad-lib* is to speak a line of your own, a line the writer of the play did not include. In certain situations the author of a play may suggest that several people talk at the same time. Sometimes this type of conversation is intended to last until a certain task has been performed by a principal actor. If, for example, several children are waiting for Santa Claus, the printed script might run like this:

FIRST CHILD. When is Santa coming?

SECOND CHILD. What will he bring?

OTHER CHILDREN (*all speaking at the same time*). I want a doll. I want a truck. I want a bike.

Now, if Santa fails to appear in the play at the right moment, the children will need to continue the dialogue in their own way: "I think Santa is late." "Well, he has lots to do," and so on.

Sometimes an actor forgets a line. When this happens other actors must keep the play moving by saying something appropriate until the speaker is either prompted or remembers what he should say.

Any lines that are ad-libbed must be in character. Do not, for example, use the speech of the 1970's in a colonial play. If you really understand your part and if you are every inch an actor, you will never fall into that out-of-character trap.

The voice is like a musical organ. It can produce a wide range of tones with many levels of volume. A voice carries best when an actor speaks from his diaphragm, not from his throat. The diaphragm is a dome-shaped sheet of muscle and tissue at the base of the chest. To feel the action of your diaphragm, place your hands below your chest. Breathe deeply, and then exhale slowly. You can feel your diaphragm inflate and deflate.

Sometimes a beginning actor cannot finish a line for the simple reason that he runs out of breath before he reaches the last word. The last word may be the most important word in the sentence.

Practice saying your lines aloud. Practice voice control as you learn your lines. Decide for yourself when you need to take a deep breath in order to say a sentence effectively.

Memorize lines quickly. They are your lines. Make the most of them. The success of the whole production may depend on you, regardless of the size of the role you are playing.

Onstage

Professional actors spend years developing theatrical technique, methods of acting that help them portray characters in a most dramatic manner. Mastering a few of these techniques will help you put across the spirit and the message of your play in an artistic way.

Listen to your director and try to carry out his or her suggestions. Even if you do not have an adult director, learn and use the basic acting techniques that follow.

Frame a picture. At every moment during a play, the stage is a picture frame, and the actors are persons in that picture. Usually at the first rehearsal the director of the play "blocks out" each scene; that is, he tells each character where to stand or sit. The director's job is made easier when all characters help him keep the stage picture artistic.

The picture must be kept in balance. At no time should a group of actors gather on one side of the stage, leaving the other side empty.

Every actor should be seen unless he is purposely hiding. Each player must avoid standing in front of or behind another actor.

Never cross in front of a person who is speaking unless there is a special reason to call attention to the act.

Standing and sitting. Learn to stand at ease with the weight of your body evenly divided, your chest out, your shoulders back, and your hands at your sides. This is an excellent habit whether you are performing or not. And, of course, if you feel the character you are portraying would stand differently then act accordingly. For example, a man who in some ways resembles Prince Philip of the United Kingdom might stand as the prince often is pictured—erect, feet together, and hands clasped behind his back. A cowboy might stand as the late Will Rogers stood: feet apart, head bent slightly to one side. An old man might lean on a cane.

Actors speaking to one another do not as a rule face directly. Each stands at a slight angle and throws his voice to the corner he is facing at the back of the auditorium. When he is in this position, the audience can see the expression on his face and, if he speaks loudly enough and clearly enough, can hear each word.

The same arrangement exists for actors who are talking to each other while seated. Their chairs are placed at an angle so that the audience can see the expression on their faces and hear what they are saying.

This does not mean that two actors never face each other while speaking. Two men carrying a table and grumbling as they do so must look directly at each other as they speak. In a case like this, pantomime may be more important than individual words.

Sitting is as important as standing. A poor posture on the part of an actor can spoil the stage picture. Girls must learn to sit in a ladylike manner with knees together and the toe of one foot resting against the heel and instep of the other foot.

A person who is seated must be prepared to stand quickly without losing his balance. An elderly character may take hold of the arms of a chair, but a younger person must practice standing without assistance.

Gestures. Learn to use your hands in a meaningful way. Avoid all distracting gestures and mannerisms that are not in keeping with the character you are playing. When playing a background, or minor, character keep your hands in your lap or do something that is inconspicuous. For example, a woman might be knitting, but she should not pretend to drop a stitch and throw a tantrum if she has to ravel what she has done. A man or woman might pick up a book and look at it, glancing up now and then as the speaker says something interesting, but he must not call attention to himself by slamming shut the book unless the play requires that he show some reaction to the speaker. A background player might put his arm on a table as he listens, but he should not tap the table with his fingers or fidget unless there is reason to call attention to these actions.

When gesturing, put your character's ideas and speech to work at the same time. For example, if you have a line such as, "I said 'Go!' " you might say, "I said—" and then pause as you bring your arm across your chest; then, with a quick thrust of your arm, point to the door and really yell, "GO!" Practice all your lines with gestures before a mirror to perfect your timing and to produce the most effective stage picture.

Take your places. Keep in mind the play as a whole as you practice your part bit by bit. Work with the director and the other actors to keep the production moving. Speed up the dialogue in certain places. Slow it down where the script and the meaning demand. Make every line, every gesture, every bit of action lead to the climax—the high point of the play.

Curtain going up. No matter what part you are playing, big or small, remember that your part is important to the success of the play. Feel your part. Stay in character. Be every inch an actor every minute.

PUPPET PLAYS

A puppet can have a personality. There are at least three ways in which the puppeteer, the person who moves or handles the puppet, can give it remarkable personality: (1) by the way in which he constructs and dresses the puppet, (2) by the way he moves or handles the puppet, and (3) by the way he uses his own voice to interpret the voice of the puppet.

Of these three the voice is the most important. Every puppet should be given a voice which expresses his attitude and his mood, a voice which will tell the audience what kind of person this puppet is. Although in a group of puppets one may be bouncing up and down to indicate he is speaking, it is not the movement alone that helps the audience to distinguish one puppet from another. The voice is most important.

The puppeteer must make his voice reach the last person in the audience. This is not always easy because those handling the puppets must speak through some kind of barrier, a curtain or some other device which hides the puppeteers from the audience.

Be careful in choosing your barrier. It is easier to speak through a bedsheet, crepe paper, or other thin material than through a cardboard wall or a cage-like puppet theater.

A few hints will help you project your voice. Do not crouch behind a puppet theater. Stand—or at least sit up straight or kneel—so you can breathe deeply and thereby increase the volume of your voice without straining.

Read the whole play carefully and then mark the key lines (see page 22). The audience must be able to hear and understand every word in these important lines in order to catch the point of the play. Say these key lines especially clearly, slowly, and loudly.

Memorize your lines. Don't read them. You will find it much easier to project your voice when speaking than when reading. When lines are read, the reader is inclined to lower his head and let his voice drop. It is easier to pick up the cues of other players, or puppeteers, when lines have been memorized and it is not necessary to watch a printed page. And certainly when lines are said from memory the puppeteer then can give greater attention to the action of the puppet.

When your lines have been memorized, practice saying them over aloud, slowly and with expression. Remember an audience cannot read a puppet's lips. It can get no clues from the puppet's facial expressions and few from bodily movements. The spoken word is all important in a puppet play.

If possible, rehearse the play in the room where the production will be given. Ask someone to check to be sure that people at the back of the room can hear the lines of the play and see the puppets when the audience is seated. In a large stageless room it is best to have puppet action three or four feet above the floor so that the seated audience looks up to see the puppets.

Over-the-Wall Puppet Theater

One of the easiest puppet theaters to construct, and one of the most satisfactory, is an "over-the-wall" type. String a clothesline across a stage; or, in the case of an outdoor show, tie the clothesline between trees. Hang sheets or crepe paper over the line to hide the puppeteers from the audience.

If the line is high enough, puppeteers may stand as they speak and work the puppets above the line. If the line is long enough, a number of puppets can appear onstage at the same time. This is advantageous in plays where a group of puppets sing together, or appear in a mob scene or at a dance or other gathering.

A draped coatrack or any other piece of equipment about four feet high can be used in place of a draped clothesline. Of if the play calls for a wall or a fence and you want to be realistic, construct it of cardboard and paint it.

Any type of puppet may be used with an over-the-wall theater, but the two-bag puppets described here are easy to make and effective.

Two-Bag Puppets

A two-bag puppet has a head, shoulders, and a body. Therefore he looks quite a bit like a real actor. To make one you will need the following:

2 paper bags of different sizes; for example, one bag about 6 inches wide and 8 inches long and another bag about 8 inches wide and 12 inches long.

construction paper
paste
masking tape
twig or other stick about 6 inches long

The smaller bag forms the head and neck of the puppet. The larger bag forms the body. Cut a three-inch slot in the bottom of the larger bag. Insert the open end of the smaller bag, gathering the bottom to make it fit into the slot. Fasten the bags together with masking tape. Place a twig or other small stick in the center of the back of the puppet, over the place where the two bags are joined. Hold the twig in place with masking tape.

At this point, to see how the puppet will work, place your arm inside the lower bag with your center finger extending into the upper bag. Lower your fingers to make your puppet nod and move his head as he speaks—that is, as you speak for him.

Now turn the puppet into a character, a person or an animal, by giving him a face and suitable clothing. Cut eyes, nose, mouth, and even hair if you like, from construction paper and paste them on the smaller bag.

Decorate the lower, larger bag with buttons, bows, belt, or other accessories. Or draw on construction paper and cut out a dress or a man's suit, uniform, or other suitable costume and paste it on the larger bag.

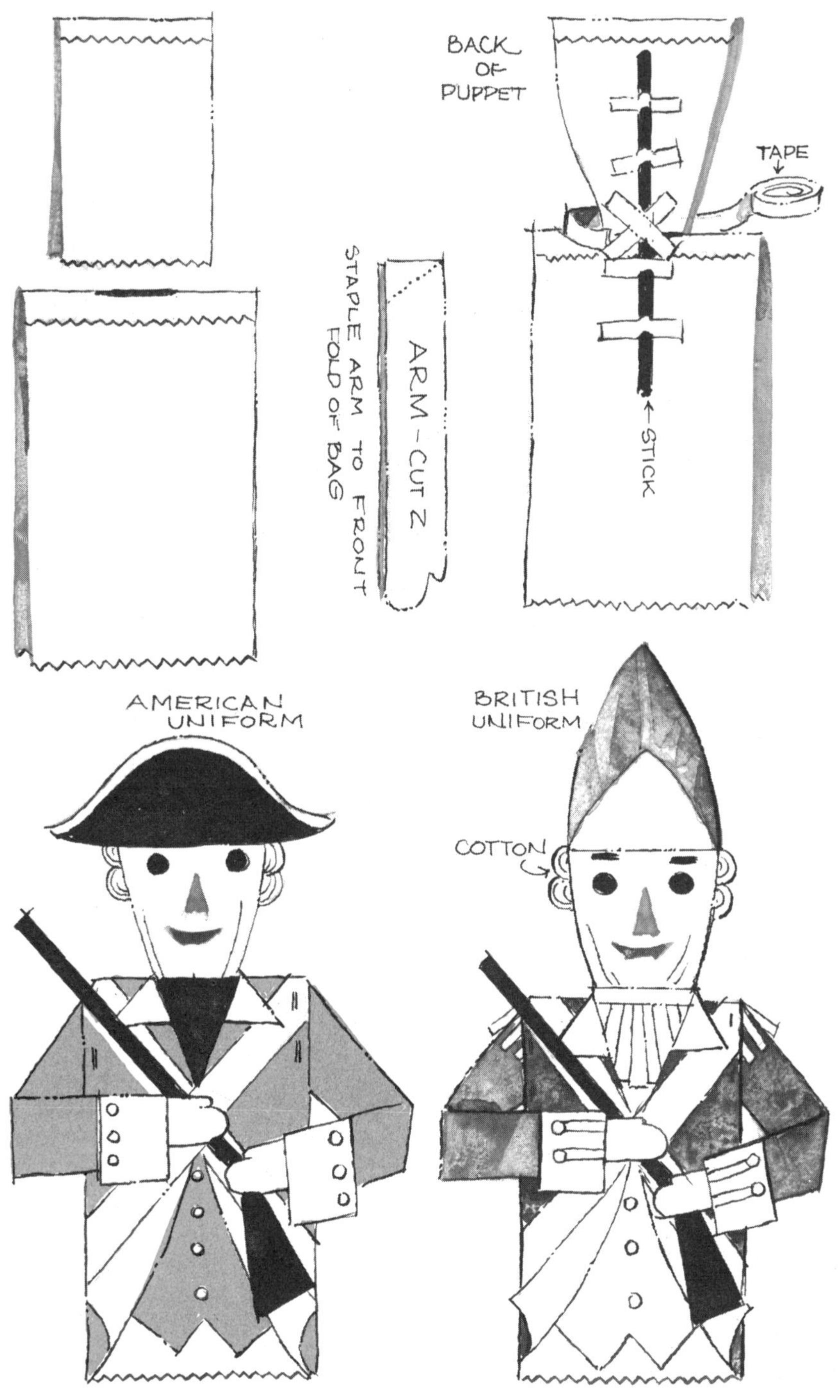
BACK OF PUPPET
TAPE
STICK
ARM-CUT 2
STAPLE ARM TO FRONT FOLD OF BAG
AMERICAN UNIFORM
BRITISH UNIFORM
COTTON

PLAY A PART

WHO WILL BE KING?

Introduction

How do you say "oh" when you are surprised? How do you say "oh" when you are disgusted? You are just like the princess and the maidens in this play. The tones of their voices indicate how they feel. When they are surprised they say "oh, oh, oh" with wonderment. When they are disgusted they say "oh" in quite a different way. Their song is quick and happy.

Ugly Creature has a deep, ugly voice. At least it must be very different from the voices of the princess and her maidens. Ugly Creature must not, however, speak in grunts. The audience must be able to hear and understand each line, especially the punch line, "I got more kisses that way."

Who Will Be King? may be produced with four characters—Princess Rosemarie, Ugly Creature, and two Fair Maidens—or, in an over-the-wall puppet theater (see page 33), with as many fair maidens as can be managed above the wall.

The wall may be constructed by hanging any sheet over a clothesline strung across a stage. However, green or flowered sheets, or green crepe paper will help to give the impression that the princess and the maidens are dancing in the park.

Use any kind of puppets—two-bag puppets (see page 34), bag-head puppets, fist puppets, stick puppets, or marionettes. Make the princess and the maidens as pretty as possible with brightly colored dresses.

Ugly Creature may be a monster with enormous eyes and ears made of tree leaves, with a wide mouth and big teeth, or he may simply be a boy with straggly hair hanging down over his eyes.

Characters

PRINCESS ROSEMARIE — UGLY CREATURE
FAIR MAIDENS — TWO CHILDREN

SCENE. Princess Rosemarie *and* Fair Maidens *are singing and dancing to the tune of* "Lavender Blue."

PRINCESS ROSEMARIE *and*
FAIR MAIDENS. Girls like to sing,
Diddle, diddle,
Bells like to ring.

PRINCESS ROSEMARIE. I shall be queen,

ALL. Diddle, diddle,
Who will be king?

PRINCESS ROSEMARIE. That's the problem. Who will be king?

FAIR MAIDEN 1. That's easy. When you are queen, your husband will be king.

PRINCESS. I know; but where can I find a prince to marry me?

OTHERS. We don't know.

MAIDEN 2. All the princes are too old.

MAIDEN 3. Or too young.

OTHERS (*sadly*). Oh-oh-oh.

MAIDEN 3. You could be a princess in distress.

PRINCESS ROSEMARIE. Why distress?

MAIDEN 3. Because then an unknown prince could rescue you.

OTHERS. No-o-o—

MAIDEN 4. You could find a prince in distress.

ROSEMARIE. Why a prince in distress?

MAIDEN 4. Then you could rescue him.

OTHERS. No-o-o.

MAIDEN 5. I know. You could find a prince in disguise.

PRINCESS ROSEMARIE. How could I do that?

MAIDEN 5. It's easy. Find an ugly creature. (*Others nod.*)

PRINCESS ROSEMARIE. Yes, go on.

MAIDEN 5. Then you say, "Ugly Creature, are you a prince in disguise?" (*Others nod.*)

PRINCESS ROSEMARIE. Yes, go on.

MAIDEN 5. Then if he says "yes," you kiss him.

OTHERS. Oh-oh-oh!

MAIDEN 5. Then he turns into a prince, and you marry him.

OTHERS. Oh-oh-oh!

PRINCESS ROSEMARIE. Maybe you are right. The world is full of ugly creatures. One could be a prince.

OTHERS (*nodding*). Yes, one could be a prince!

PRINCESS ROSEMARIE. Let's sing again.

ALL. Girls like to sing,
Diddle, diddle,
Bells like to ring.

PRINCESS ROSEMARIE. I shall be queen,

ALL. Diddle, diddle,
Who will be king?

(Ugly Creature *pops up in the middle of the stage, next to* Princess Rosemarie.)

PRINCESS ROSEMARIE. Hi, beautiful!

UGLY CREATURE. No one ever called me beautiful before.

PRINCESS ROSEMARIE. But you are beautiful! (*Others nod as*

she pauses.) You are beautiful inside. You are really a prince in disguise.

(Ugly Creature *wags his head.*)

FAIR MAIDENS. Oh-oh-oh.

PRINCESS ROSEMARIE. You are a prince, aren't you? (Ugly Creature *wags his head, back and forth, not saying* "yes" *or* "no.")

PRINCESS ROSEMARIE. I am going to find out if you are a prince in disguise.

UGLY CREATURE. How?

PRINCESS ROSEMARIE. I am going to kiss you.

FAIR MAIDENS. Oh-oh-oh.

UGLY CREATURE. OK, I'm willing.

(Princess Rosemarie *bends over slowly and kisses* Ugly Creature *with a loud smack.*)

UGLY CREATURE. Thanks!

(Princess Rosemarie *backs away a little and pauses a second.*)

PRINCESS ROSEMARIE. Nothing happened.

FAIR MAIDENS. No-o-o—

UGLY CREATURE. Try again. (Princess Rosemarie *again leans over and kisses* Ugly Creature *with a loud smack.*) Thanks!

(Princess Rosemarie *backs away a little and pauses.*)

PRINCESS ROSEMARIE. Nothing happened.

FAIR MAIDEN. No-o-o—

UGLY CREATURE. Try again. (Princess Rosemarie *again bends over and kisses* Ugly Creature *with a loud smack.*) Thanks!

(Princess Rosemarie *backs away and pauses.*)

PRINCESS ROSEMARIE (*angrily*). Nothing happened! You are not a prince in disguise!

UGLY CREATURE (*shaking head*). No.

PRINCESS ROSEMARIE. Why didn't you tell me?

UGLY CREATURE (*bobbing up and down excitedly*). I got more kisses this way. (*Pops down behind scene.*)

PRINCESS ROSEMARIE and FAIR MAIDENS (*in disgust*). Oh-oh—

FAIR MAIDEN 1. Let's sing again.

ALL. Girls like to sing,
Diddle, diddle,
Bells like to ring.

PRINCESS ROSEMARIE. I shall be queen,

ALL. Diddle, diddle,

(*Words spoken*) He—won't be—king!

UGLY CREATURE (*popping up at end of line*). No. But thanks for the kisses.

PRINCESS ROSEMARIE and FAIR MAIDENS (*in disgust*). Oh! (Ugly Creature *pops down. Others move quickly down the line, as if chasing him, and disappear one by one.*)

(*Two children appear as* Maidens *are leaving.*)

FIRST CHILD. What a phony fairy tale! The Princess didn't catch a prince.

SECOND CHILD. No, but she will! Some day! She will!

ROBIN HOOD MEETS LITTLE JOHN

Introduction

An old-fashioned way of speaking does not keep Robin Hood and Little John from bragging. Each line is said loudly and very clearly. The Merry Men, proud of their leader, sing with gusto. Little John and Robin Hood must look and sound as if they are having a real fight; but they must not damage the puppets, and they must not fight so long they delay the play. Two or three stout blows are enough.

There are three main characters in this play plus several of Robin Hood's Merry Men. One additional person will be needed to act as announcer, or narrator, to describe the scenes for the audience.

If an over-the-wall theater is used (see page 33), cover the lower part with thin green cloth or green crepe paper so that standing puppeteers can be heard easily. For the second scene, the announcer may simply emphasize that there is a log across a stream and let the audience imagine the scene, or a log may be made of cardboard, attached to a lath, and held by two puppeteers.

If you would like Robin Hood and the Merry Men to wear traditional Robin Hood hats, stuff slightly the head of a two-bag puppet. Make green hats of construction paper. Fasten them on the puppets with gummed or masking tape. Little John traditionally wears rough hunting clothes; his hat might be a small round cap, cut from dark brown or black construction paper.

Characters

NARRATOR	
ROBIN HOOD	LITTLE JOHN
WILL SCARLET	OTHER MERRY MEN

SCENE I. (*To be read by* Narrator). Sherwood Forest where dwell Robin Hood and his Merry Men amid the mighty oaks. They are singing!

ROBIN HOOD and MERRY MEN. (Robin *has a horn attached to his belt and a stick in his hand. He and his men are singing to the tune of* "Pop! Goes the Weasel.")

Oh, Robin is a very fine man,
The finest we have seen-o!
He lives in Sherwood with his band
'Mong the leaves so green-o!

ROBIN HOOD. Well sung! I've not seen sport for fourteen days. I shall now go forth and seek adventure.

WILL SCARLET. Let me go with you.

ROBIN HOOD. Nay, I'll go alone. Tarry in the greenwood. Listen well. If you hear three blasts from my horn, come at once.

MERRY MEN. Aye, Robin! We will! (*Exit* Robin. Merry Men *repeat song.*)

Oh, Robin is a very fine man,
The finest we have seen-o!
He lives in Sherwood with his band
'Mong the leaves so green-o!

SCENE II. (*To be read by* Narrator). A fallen log spans a stream in Sherwood Forest, and there Robin Hood meets Little John.

(Robin Hood *enters left and* Little John *right. They stand on opposite ends of the log.*)

ROBIN HOOD. Stand back and let the better man cross!

LITTLE JOHN. Stand back yourself. I am the better man, I am.

ROBIN HOOD. We'll see. Cross that log and I'll crack your ribs with my cudgel!

LITTLE JOHN. Cross and I'll tan your hide!

ROBIN HOOD. Stand back! I'm coming.

LITTLE JOHN. I await your coming. (*They meet in the middle of the log ad fight. At last* Robin *tumbles off the log and disappears below the puppet stage.*)

LITTLE JOHN (*looking down*). Where are you now, fine stranger?

ROBIN HOOD (*below stage*). In the flood, and floating. Give me your hand, fine fellow.

LITTLE JOHN. Gladly. (*He bends down to help* Robin. *Just then three blasts of a horn are heard.*) What's that?

ROBIN HOOD (*standing on log*). My horn to call my Merry Men.

LITTLE JOHN. Merry Men? You must be Robin Hood.

ROBIN HOOD. Indeed I am.

(*Enter* Merry Men *saying,* "Robin Hood, are you all right? Shall we throw him in?" *and so on.*)

ROBIN HOOD (*yelling above their voices*). Stand back! I want you to meet a right good man and true. What do men call you?

LITTLE JOHN. People call me John Little.

WILL SCARLET. You mean Little John, small and sinewy.

ROBIN HOOD. Well, John Little, or Little John, would you like to join our band?

LITTLE JOHN. Indeed I would!

OTHERS. Yea, for Little John!

WILL SCARLET. Come, let's sing.

ALL. Oh, Robin is a very fine man,
The finest we have seen-o!
He lives in Sherwood with his band,
'Mong the leaves so green-o!

TRAILING ARBUTUS

Introduction

The old man in this puppet play speaks in a low, cold voice. The young man speaks in a clear, eager voice. In addition to the two characters and the storyteller, a white flower also makes an appearance on the puppet stage but has no lines to say.

For this production almost any kind of puppet can be used and almost any kind of puppet stage. The easiest puppet to make would be a cardboard figure attached to a lath so it could appear over any kind of barrier.

Characters

STORYTELLER	YOUNG MAN
OLD MAN	WHITE FLOWER (*trailing arbutus*)

SCENE. A clear spot in the North Woods.

STORYTELLER. The Indians of the North Woods have a legend about the trailing arbutus, the first flower to appear each year in the northern hemisphere. The scene of our play is a clear spot in the North Woods. When the play is over, we should like our audience to guess who the young man is and who the old man is.

OLD MAN (*chanting*). I bring frost; I bring snow.
I bring cold, wherever I go.

YOUNG MAN (*entering*). Well, hello. You look miserable. May I help you?

OLD MAN. Help me? Help me? Young man, you just don't know how powerful I am.

YOUNG MAN. Maybe you are right. What can you do?

OLD MAN. I make lakes and rivers as hard as stone. Can you do that?

YOUNG MAN. Just the opposite. I make rivers rush along and lakes ripple from shore to shore.

OLD MAN. Ha! I make leaves fall from the trees.

YOUNG MAN. I make trees burst into bud.

OLD MAN. When I come, birds fly south. Animals crawl into dens.

YOUNG MAN. When I come, birds come too. They fill the sky. Sleeping animals wake up.

OLD MAN. Where I walk, no flowers can bloom.

YOUNG MAN. Flowers bloom everywhere soon after I arrive.

OLD MAN. Look, why don't you go away? I've been here a long time. I think I'll stay awhile. I'm very strong—

YOUNG MAN. Not strong enough, I think. I'm sure my friends, the birds, the flowers, and the rippling streams, will help me. When I return, they always follow. (*The top portion of the white flower begins to show above the barrier.*)

OLD MAN. Who are you, young man? What is happening to my power? I'm going away from here before we start to fight. Good day, sir! (*Exits.*)

YOUNG MAN. Goodbye, old man. Now, what is this? My little snow-white flower, edged in pink. (*The flower now shows completely above the barrier.*) I salute you once again, Trailing Arbutus, always the first to greet me!

STORYTELLER. Can you guess who the old man is?

AUDIENCE. Winter.

STORYTELLER. Can you guess who the young man is?

AUDIENCE. Spring.

STORYTELLER. You are right. Thank you for listening to the legend of the seasons.

PLAY A PART

HAPPY NESTING

Introduction

In this play, which takes place in the springtime, the characters are all birds, chatting happily on a fence or wall. When Mrs. Owl speaks she draws out the "oo" as an owl would sound its "Who-o-o-o." Other birds should seem to chirp, but each spoken word must come out clearly and distinctly.

There are nine speaking parts, but as many other birds as are practical may take part. If the fence or wall is long enough, and if there are enough players, the chorus should include both father and mother birds perched on the fence. If a small group is putting on the play, then use only those birds with speaking parts.

Boys as well as girls can operate mother-bird puppets and speak their lines. As each bird speaks, the puppeteer bobs that puppet up and down.

Any kind of barrier may be used (see page 31) as the fence in this production. A painted scene of a picket fence or a stone wall would be effective. Because the puppets stay in one place on the fence when they are visible above the barrier, the puppeteers may be seated behind the fence or wall.

Simple stick puppets may be made by cutting out and coloring large pictures of the birds in the play. Mrs. Cowbird, who is to make her appearance in the middle of the row of birds on the fence, should have a front-view picture. Half the other birds should face left and half should face right. Mount the pictures on long strips of cardboard or on lathes so that they may be held above the fence or wall.

If you would like to use loop puppets, follow the directions for making them given at the end of this play. Loop puppets are fun to make and give more lasting importance to the production of the play.

The birds' song may be sung to the tune of an old Bavarian

folksong (see melody at the end of the play) or to any tune which goes well with the words.

Characters

MRS. ORIOLE	MRS. SPARROW	MRS. COWBIRD
MRS. ROBIN	MRS. OWL	MRS. MEADOWLARK
MRS. VIREO	MRS. BLUEJAY	MRS. SWALLOW
		OTHER BIRDS

SCENE. *A long fence in the springtime. Many kinds of birds, but not the cowbird, are singing together. Their song may be sung to the tune given at the end of this play.*

ALL BIRDS. Cheery, cheery, cheery! Time to nest.
Every mother bird likes her nest best.
And as we are building we shall sing,
"Cheery, cheery, cheery! It is spring!"

MRS. ORIOLE. My! It's good to be back and nesting again. I have a perfect place for my nest. A tall willow tree. I can just see my little basket swinging in the breeze.

MRS. ROBIN. I know you love your swinging nest, Mrs. Oriole, and I like my nest in the peach tree. But I have a problem.

Mrs. Sparrow. I know, Mrs. Robin, I know.

Mrs. Vireo. So do I, Mrs. Robin. Mrs. Sparrow and I know. We have the same problem.

Mrs. Owl. True-oo-oo-oo! We have problems, all of us. But you, Mrs. Robin, Mrs. Sparrow, Mrs. Vireo, tell me about your problem.

Mrs. Robin. It is commonly known.

Mrs. Sparrow. It really isn't gossip.

Mrs. Vireo. She does it every year.

Mrs. Owl. Who-o-o-o-o? And what does she do?

Mrs. Robin, Mrs. Sparrow, Mrs. Vireo. MRS. COWBIRD!

Mrs. Robin. Mrs. Cowbird is the only bird that does not build her own nest.

Mrs. Sparrow. Mrs. Cowbird always lays eggs in the nest of a smaller bird.

Mrs. Vireo. Mrs. Cowbird deserts her young. She expects us to bring up her babies along with our own.

Mrs. Swallow. I think something should be done. Mrs. Owl, would it help if we talked to Mrs. Cowbird?

Mrs. Owl. Who-o-o-o knows? Who-o-o-o knows?

Mrs. Bluejay. Scolding won't help. I do that often.

Mrs. Robin. Maybe her problem is ignorance. Let's tell her how we build our nests. Do you think she will follow our example?

Mrs. Owl. Who-o-o-o knows? There are many kinds of nests. She might like to build one. Who-o-o-o knows?

Mrs. Sparrow. Here she comes now. Let's try to talk to her. (Mrs. Cowbird *perches on fence.*)

Mrs. Cowbird. Good morning! Good morning! How are all of you this splendid spring morning?

All Birds. Fine, thank you, Mrs. Cowbird.

Mrs. Robin. Mrs. Cowbird, we are getting ready to build our nests.

Mrs. Cowbird. Good! Good! Good!

MRS. SPARROW. We want to tell you, Mrs. Cowbird, how we build our nests.

MRS. COWBIRD. Very interesting. Do tell.

MRS. ROBIN. I choose a flat place or a crotch in a tree. Then I gather mud and grass and mix them and shape them into a nest.

MRS. COWBIRD. Mrs. Robin, I think you make a lovely nest!

MRS. ORIOLE. I am Mrs. Oriole, Mrs. Cowbird. You may not know me as well as you know Mrs. Robin. My nest is unusual. I choose a tall tree. Then I make a hanging cradle. To do this I weave together different kinds of plants and string.

MRS. COWBIRD. I never tried a swinging nest. Sounds delightful!

MRS. MEADOWLARK. I am Mrs. Meadowlark. I rather like a ranch type nest built in a slight dip in the ground. I make my nest of grasses, and then arch other grasses over the top like a dome.

MRS. COWBIRD. The dome sounds lovely.

MRS. SWALLOW. I am Mrs. Swallow. Mrs. Barn Swallow, that is. I make a nest in a barn up next to the rafters. I gather mud and grasses and cement them together with saliva. Then I line the nest with feathers.

MRS. COWBIRD. How cozy it must be!

MRS. ROBIN. We have told you about many kinds of nests, Mrs. Cowbird.

MRS. COWBIRD. Oh, yes, you have. Thank you!

MRS. SPARROW. Do you think you would like to build a nest of your own?

MRS. COWBIRD. A nest of my own? Think of that. A nest of my own? Just think of it.

MRS. VIREO. Yes, please *do* think of it.

ALL BIRDS (*except* Mrs. Cowbird). Mrs. Cowbird, please build a nest of your own.

MRS. COWBIRD. Well, well. I'll think about it. Happy nesting, all of you. (*Disappears from fence.*)

PLAY A PART

Mrs. Robin. Well, Mrs. Owl, do you think that Mrs. Cowbird will build a nest of her own?

Mrs. Owl. Who-o-o-o knows? She never has. Who-o-o-o knows? She never has.

Mrs. Oriole. I suppose there are some things you just can't change.

Mrs. Robin. Since that is true, let's sing. After all, it *is* spring.

Birds. Cheery, cheery, cheery in the spring.
All the little birds begin to sing.
If you only listen you can hear,
"Cheery, cheery, cheery! Spring is here."

Loop Bird-Puppets

Materials

construction paper in the colors of a bird
thin straight stick, 12 to 20 inches long,
the length depending on the length of the finished puppet
glue
facial tissue or very thin tissue paper
paste
staples

Select construction paper the color of the back of a given bird. Cut a strip about two inches wide the length of the construction-paper sheet. If the breast of the bird is a different color from the back, then, using paper the color of the breast, cut a strip two inches wide and about one-half the length of the construction-paper sheet. For example, for a robin cut a long strip of brown paper, two inches wide, the length of the construction paper, and a red strip two inches wide but about one-half the length of the brown strip. Paste the shorter strip over the longer one (so that when dried, one end of the strip will be one color and the other end another color). For a robin, paste the red strip on top of the brown one, so that the red extends from the end of the strip to about the middle.

Overlap the ends of the long strip, making an oblong loop, and staple the ends together to form the body of the bird.

Select paper the principal color of the head of the bird. Cut a strip of paper two inches wide and about three-fourths as long as the original long strip cut for the body. Overlap the ends of the strip (to form a circle) for the head, and staple the ends together. Staple the head of the bird onto the body.

If the bird has a small bill, cut a one-inch square, of yellow paper. Fold diagonally across the center to form two triangles. Put paste or glue on the back of one of the triangles and press it onto the head where the bill should be. If the bird should have a longer bill, cut a diamond shape in an appropriate size from construction paper and fold in half across the middle of the width. Put paste or glue on one of the folded sides and position on the bird's head.

Cut eyes from the construction paper and paste them to the head. Cut yellow claw-feet and paste them at the bottom of the large body loop.

If the bird being constructed has a topknot, cut from paper of an appropriate color a triangle measuring about two inches on each side; slash the edges on two sides. On the third side, fold under approximately one-fourth inch, apply glue or paste to this folded base, and position the topknot on the bird's head.

Choose paper the color of the bird's wings. Fold a piece in half. Using the fold as the center of the wingspread, draw a wing. Cut out double wings, cutting through both folds of the paper and being careful not to cut through the folded edge itself. Paste or staple the wings to the back of the bird.

If the bird has markings on its head, wings, or body, either paint them on or cut them from paper and paste in place.

Insert the stick through the center of the bottom of the bird and up through the place where the two loops (body and head) are joined. Moisten a small piece of tissue with glue. Make it into a small wad. Just below the spot where the bottom loop touches the stick, press the wad around the stick and onto the loop as well. Put a small wad of the sticky paper above and below each place where the stick touches a loop of paper. Let dry. These little wads of paper are intended to prevent the puppet from sliding up or down the stick while it is being handled in the play. Gummed tape, properly attached to both stick and loops, may serve the same purpose.

Variation

To make a larger loop bird-puppet, for use in an auditorium, simply use oversize construction paper. Cut the body the length of the paper and the head about three-fourths the length of the paper. Both body and head should be about three inches wide.

—*Happy Nesting* is based on play and puppet designs by Marie Wilt. Used with permission.

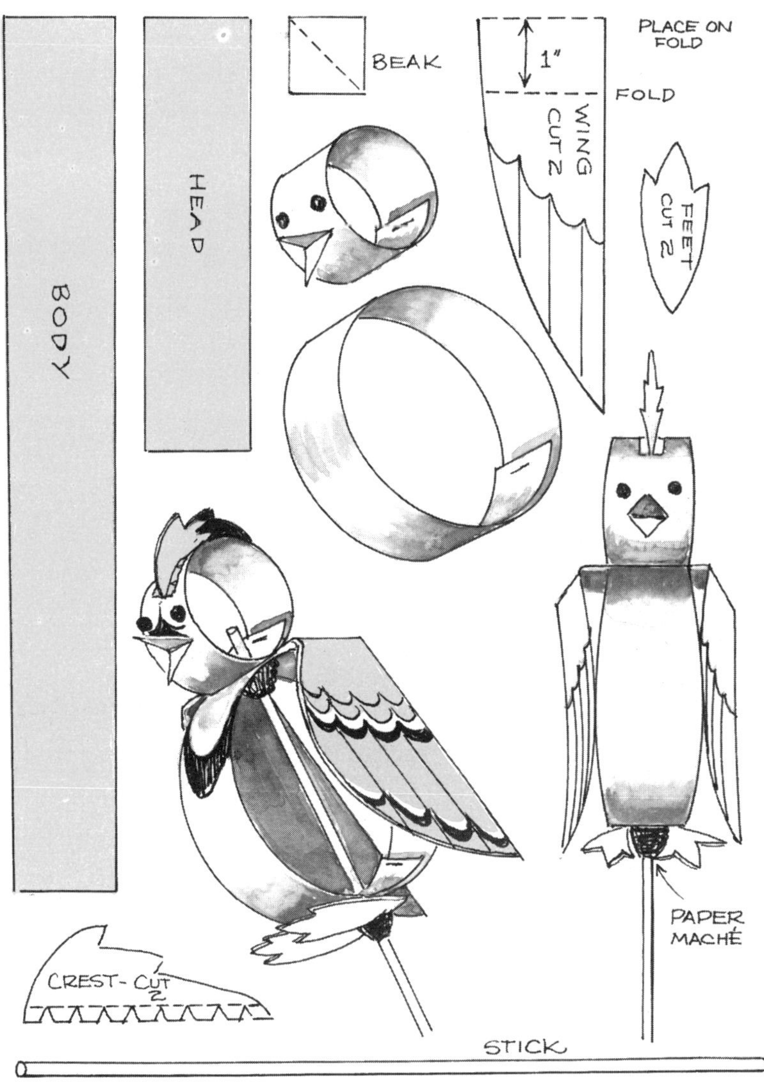

PLAY A PART

THE GOLDEN SPIKE

Introduction

In this play, the actors or puppeteers who act and speak for the puppets must pretend they are earthworms living in a tunnel underneath Promontory Point, Utah, on that day in 1869 when the first continental railroad was dedicated. If you had never seen a train, how would you feel about having one run overhead? Puzzled? Disgusted? Excited? Happy? Earthworms in this puppet skit have all of these reactions. Puppeteers must express them with their voices.

The lines about the railroads must be spoken slowly and clearly. Lem and Zeke are trying to explain the new situation to old Granny, so that she can understand why the event is important. If the characters can make Granny understand, then the audience also will understand. Offstage noises must be timed perfectly.

The skit may be put on with only the main characters, or there may be as many earthworms as can be used on the stage. The extra earthworms must react to speeches by nodding or shaking their heads or making exclamations that will not slow up the skit.

If you have a good idea about how to construct earthworm puppets, create your own; or make a puppet like the one described at the end of this play.

If this skit is being presented before a small audience, such as your class, group of playground friends, Brownie troop, Cub pack, or family, just pretend there is a golden spike in the ceiling of the tunnel. However, if you wish, you can make a simple stage that represents a tunnel. Suspend two curtains or barriers across your stage (see page 31). The top of one curtain, the front one, should be slightly lower, perhaps twelve inches lower, than the curtain in back of it. There should be ample room between the two curtains to permit the puppeteers to move freely. At the proper time the golden spike may be suspended from, or fastened over, the wire that holds the back curtain.

If you have a large cardboard puppet stage and want to use it limit the number of players to three earthworms. Combine the lines of Lem and Zeke so they are said by one player. Suspend the spike from the top of the cardboard stage so that it can be lowered at the correct time.

Characters

LEM EARTHWORM	YOUNG 'UN EARTHWORM
ZEKE EARTHWORM	OTHER EARTHWORMS
GRANNY EARTHWORM	NARRATOR

SCENE. (*To be described for the audience by the* Narrator.) The tunnel of a group of earthworms beneath Promontory Point, Utah, May 19, 1869. As the scene opens, all of the earthworms are singing and dancing.

EARTHWORMS. (*Dancing and singing to the tune of* "Turkey in the Straw.")

Do you think that an earthworm
Can dance beneath the ground?
Bow to his partner,
And turn himself around;

Bow to the left
And bow to the right,
Then jig up and down
With all his might?
Oh-oh, yes, I know an earthworm
Can dance beneath the ground.
Bow to his partner
And turn himself around.
Bow to his left
And bow to his right,
Then jig up and down
With all his might.
Yeah! (*Noise of hammers is heard offstage.*)

GRANNY. Land o' Goshen! There goes that noise again. What can it be?

LEM. I told you, Granny. Twenty thousand men are laying eight miles of track a day.

GRANNY. Track? What for, Lem?

LEM. For a train, they say.

GRANNY. Train? What's that?

LEM. I don't know. Never saw one.

GRANNY. Zeke, do you know what a train is? (*All earthworms shake their heads.*)

ZEKE. No, Granny, but one is coming from the East.

LEM. And one is coming from the West.

YOUNG 'UN. What'll happen when they meet?

LEM. They are going to stop. And someone is going to drive a golden spike into the ground right here at Promontory Point. That golden spike will join the two railroads.

GRANNY. Railroads. I thought you said *train.* (*Speaks seriously.*) Lem, I think you better go up on top of the earth. Go to the West, and do be careful! Find out what a train is like.

LEM. Yes, Granny. (*Exits.*)

GRANNY. And Zeke, I want you to go to the top of the earth, too. Go to the East. And do be careful! Find out what a train is like.

ZEKE. Yes, Granny. (*Exits.*)

(*Loud train whistles are heard offstage.*)

YOUNG 'UN (*jumping up and down*). I bet it's a train! A train! A train! (*Yells are heard offstage.*) What's that?

GRANNY. People. Lots of people. (*Pounding is heard offstage.*)

YOUNG 'UN. Granny, look up there. (*A spike appears in the ceiling.*)

GRANNY. Now, what's that?

YOUNG 'UN. Don't know. But it's pretty.

GRANNY. Go see what it is. Might be good to eat.

YOUNG 'UN (*stretching up to touch the spike*). Owwww. My jaw! (*Drops to stage level.*) *That's* not good to eat.

GRANNY. What's it good for?

YOUNG 'UN. I don't know. But it surely is pretty, up there on our ceiling.

LEM (*entering and speaking excitedly*). Granny! Granny! The train's a fire wagon! It runs on tracks. It came from the West. They call it Central Pacific.

GRANNY. So what?

LEM. It's full of people and cargo!

ZEKE (*entering and speaking excitedly*). Granny! Granny! The train's a fire wagon. It came from the East.

GRANNY. So what?

ZEKE. It's full of people.

GRANNY. I just can't understand what all the fuss is about.

LEM. Don't you see? It's important!

GRANNY. Why?

LEM. Because now folks can ship goods from the West Coast to the East Coast. The Central Pacific brought Japanese tea right here. Tomorrow the Union Pacific will carry that tea east all across the EN-TIRE United States.

GRANNY. Who wants tea?

ZEKE. And, Granny, the Union Pacific carried passengers. Those passengers are going to get on the Central Pacific. Now, people can travel by train across the en-tire United States.

GRANNY. Who wants to travel by train?

YOUNG 'UN. And, Granny, they drove a golden spike into the ground to join the two railroads.

GRANNY. What's important about that?

YOUNG 'UN. Don't you know, Granny?

GRANNY. No.

YOUNG 'UN. We are the only earthworms in the whole wide world who have a golden spike in the ceiling of their tunnel.

GRANNY. Now I understand. That's something to celebrate! (*Earthworms sing and dance to tune of* "Turkey in the Straw.")

FIRST GROUP OF EARTHWORMS. Oh, the Central Pacific
Was best in the West.

SECOND GROUP OF EARTHWORMS. Folks in the East
Thought the Union was best.

ALL EARTHWORMS. So they all got together
And joined the two.
Now folks can cross the country
And say "How'd you do?"
Boom de-de-ada. Boom! Boom!

GRANNY (*loudly*). Ladies and gentlemen, let me remind you. The important point is: we the earthworms of Promontory Point, Utah, are the only earthworms in the whole wide world who have a golden spike in the ceiling of their tunnel. Thank you!

OTHERS. Yeah! Yeah! (*The puppets disappear singing,* "Da, da, da" *to the tune of* "Turkey in the Straw." *Song fades out after a few measures.*)

How to Make an Earthworm Puppet

Materials

old stocking or long sock
poster paint or marking pencils
or
construction paper or aluminum foil

Put one hand and arm into an old stocking or long sock with your fingers in the toe. Close your fist. Open it slightly. As you look at your sock-covered palm, can you imagine how an earthworm would look if he were talking?

Take poster paint or marking pencils (or any colored paint that will stick to the stocking or sock you have chosen) and at the tip end of the sock, where it covers your fingernails, paint the earthworm's big upper lip. Paint his big lower lip near the base of the palm of your hand. Paint big eyes on the stocking covering your hand's middle knuckles.

When you open your fist slightly and close it again, the puppet's mouth will appear to change position as you talk for him.

If you do not want to paint features on the stocking, cut eyes and mouth from construction paper or aluminum foil and fasten them in place.

TURN SOUTH AT VOORHEES' FARM

Introduction

Boys and girls attending a playground program in Franklin Township, New Jersey, first produced this puppet play. When they sang "Yankee Doodle" and "God Save Great George, the King," and when they yelled, "The British are coming," they were reenacting the history of their own area. But each bit of history belongs to the country as a whole. Boys and girls everywhere in these United States may put on the same play with a sense of being a part of history.

This particular play may suggest an idea for one based on historical events of the area where you live. As in this one, it may be well to have one, or even two or three, narrators tell a part of the story and then let puppets act out the climax. Singing adds life to a play and permits a number of people to take part. So in planning a show based on local events, remember to include the state song, if your state has one, or songs that were popular at the time of the story.

Keep action and dialogue simple. The actions of the puppets are limited, and the voices of puppeteers carry best when sentences are short.

In *Turn South at Voorhees' Farm,* there are three primary characters along with a number of British soldiers and a number of Yankees.

Any kind of puppet may be used. See page 34 for a description of two-bag puppets. Stick puppets may be made by cutting out and coloring pictures of characters. Mount the pictures on cardboard or lath so they may be held above the barrier.

The British soldiers were known, of course, for their bright red coats. Yankees, the American revolutionists, wore whatever was available. (They are listed as Yankees in cast of characters.)

Any kind of barrier may be used (see page 31) for the puppet stage, for the narrator will have described the scene for the audience.

Have the verses of "Yankee Doodle" mimeographed and distribute them as people come to the play.

Characters

Colonel John Simcoe	Yankee Leader
British Sergeant	Other Yankees
British Soldiers	Narrator or Narrators

Scene. *Amwell Road, Franklin Township, New Jersey, 1779.*

Narrator. Today our puppeteers will re-enact a chapter of American history. The scene is the Township of Franklin, the State of New Jersey. The date: October 1779.

Before we begin our play we should like you to get into the mood of the times by singing one of the oldest truly American songs, "Yankee Doodle." But, first, let me tell you about Yankee Doodle.

Many Englishmen liked to poke fun at the American colonials by calling them Yankee Doodle dandies. The Americans didn't care one bit. They accepted the title and appropriated a British song, "Yankee Doodle." Let's all sing some of the verses.

Father and I went down to camp,
Along with Captain Gooding;
And there we see the men and boys
As thick as hasty pudding.

Chorus: Yankee Doodle, keep it up,
Yankee Doodle dandy,
Mind the music and the step,
And with the girls be handy.

And there I see a thousand men,
As rich as Squire David;
And what they wasted ev'ry day,
I wish it could be saved. (Chorus)

And there I see a little keg,
Its head all made of leather,
They knocked upon it with a club,
To call the folks together. (Chorus)

And there they'd fife away like fun,
And play on cornstalk fiddles;
And some had ribbons red as blood,
All bound around their middles. (Chorus)

Second Narrator. Please use your imagination as I describe the scene for our play, *Turn South at Voorhees' Farm.* The scene represents Amwell Road. Over here (*pointing to right*) is Brunswick, or New Brunswick, as it is called today. Many Yankees lived there. (*Yankee puppets bob up and down. The Yankee puppets are positioned off-center toward the right end of the barrier; the Redcoat puppets at first are nearer the left end.*) Over here (*pointing left*) is East Millstone, where Colonel Simcoe and his Queen's Rangers are encamped. (*Redcoat puppets bob up and down.*) The center is Middleline Road, now called South Middlebush Road. Across the street are the ashes of the Voorhees' farm and homestead which had been burned by General Cornwallis, the British commandant in 1777. (*A Yankee puppet bobs up to look at point of ashes and disappears.*)

Third Narrator. In this day of telephone, telegraph, radio, TV, and other means of communication, it is hard for us to realize that in 1779 one branch of the army didn't know what another branch of the same army had done.

General Cornwallis and his men had burned the Voorhees' farm and homestead. Colonel Simcoe, another British officer, didn't know this. Thereon hangs our tale.

The British soldiers have assembled in East Millstone and are singing their national anthem.

(*The song is sung to the tune of* "My Country 'Tis of Thee.")

All British Soldiers.

God save great George, the King;
Long live our noble King;
God save the King!
Send him victorious,
Happy and glorious,
Long to reign over us:
God save the King!

COL. SIMCOE. Attention!

SERGEANT. Attention!

COL. SIMCOE. Our plan of attack is now complete. We are to join the British regulars at South River.

SERGEANT. Do we go through Brunswick, sir? I understand that it is a nest of Yankee Doodles.

COL. SIMCOE. You are right. Brunswick is a seat of colonial sympathizers. We must avoid Brunswick. This is the plan. You will proceed down Amwell Road to Middleline Road. You will recognize it as it is opposite the Voorhees' farm and homestead. Turn right at Voorhees' farm.

SERGEANT. Yes, sir! Turn right at Voorhees' farm. Company, forward march! (*They start down road singing,* "God Save Great George, the King!")

COL. SIMCOE. Halt! There is a road going directly south. Does anyone see a homestead that might be the Voorhees' farm?

SERGEANT. There might have been a fire over there, sir.

SOLDIER. I passed here a year ago. There wasn't any house there at that time.

COL. SIMCOE. Orders are to turn south at Voorhees' farm. Must be some other road. Forward march! (*Continue marching.*)

(Yankee Leader *bobs up center stage. Rushes ahead of English. As he nears Brunswick he yells.*)

YANKEE LEADER. The British are coming! Down Amwell Road!

OTHER YANKEES. To arms! To arms! (*Start to sing* "Yankee Doodle" *as they rush down the road. Troops clash with lots of* "bang, bang, bang!"

Col. Simcoe. Retreat! (British Soldiers *who have not fallen run back down Amwell Road*).

Yankees. Hurrah! Hurrah!

First Narrator. Needless to say, those British soldiers did not join the English regulars at South River. As we all know the British lost the war. The Yankee Doodle dandies founded a new nation, the United States of America, which we are happy to say includes a very historic spot, the Township of Franklin, in the state of New Jersey.

Before you go, let us all sing the tune that the British soldiers sang, with our very own words, "My Country 'Tis of Thee."

—*Turn South at Voorhees' Farm* is based on information found on the back of the menu of Colonial Farms Restaurant, located in the house which Garrett Voorhees built in 1793 on the site of the homestead that was burned by Cornwallis.

ROCK
THE
BABY
GRANNY

SKITS

A skit is a sketch, a brief dramatization or interpretation of an event or a situation. The event or situation covers only a very short period of time, usually a matter of minutes, which means that the actions and lines of the players often must be exaggerated in order to have the audience get the point of the skit. Skits require but little rehearsal, and the number of players usually may be increased or decreased to fit the needs of the group giving the performance.

The skits in this book are dramatizations of jokes or funny situations. Each skit will be funny, when produced, if everyone in the cast works as a team to keep the show moving at a quick pace to bring the exaggerated situation to a hilarious close. The success of the show depends upon the performance of the group as a whole.

In this book each skit has a snapper line—or punch line—at the end. The punch line is extremely important. Everyone in the audience must be able to hear and understand it if they are to understand the point of the production. Therefore, each person in the cast must help to put the punch line across. The speaker who has the punch line must say it loudly and with exaggerated clarity. All other characters must listen intently and then react in an obvious manner.

Because special qualities of each character's personality must be made clear to the audience in a brief period of time, each player must understand well the nature of the person he is playing—that is, a pompous, talkative braggart; a suspicious old lady who trusts nobody; a gossip who insists on hearing and telling everything; a happy-go-lucky fellow who likes everybody; or a timid, shrinking violet afraid of her shadow. Every mannerism, every movement the player makes must express the personality of the character he is playing. For the brief time in which the skit takes place the player must be the person he is portraying.

In this kind of skit the characters are easily recognized types, something like the characters in a comic strip. They are enough like people we know to seem believable, but certain qualities are exaggerated. Every actor in the skit must take very seriously these exaggerations. Therein lies the humor of the situation. For example, see the skit "Murky Monster Foiled Again" (page 69).

The monster is all bad. There is no good in him at all. His role is to pollute the bay. The fish in the bay, before Murky Monster comes, are happy. Not one of them has an unhappy concern. The smiles on their faces and the lilt of their voices let the audience know that these are happy fish.

And then Murky Monster enters the bay. The fish are terrified. The audience may roar with laughter as Murky sweeps across the stage spreading his vile pollution in a menacing way; but Murky does not smile. This is very serious business for him. The fish tremble in terror. Gone are the happy smiles. If one fish laughs at Murky's antics, the scene will be spoiled.

Do not try to say lines while the audience is laughing loudly.

Freeze the scene for a moment, or continue to pantomime in character, while waiting for the laughter to subside. When the audience is reasonably quiet, say the next line loudly as a signal that the show is to continue.

Remember, this kind of skit must be fun. Don't let it drag. Be a certain type of person for a short time. Be completely the character the skit requires.

MURKY MONSTER FOILED AGAIN

Introduction

This skit is a spoof on those free-our-kingdom-from-the-dragon (or monster) legends. And like most such legends it contains an element of truth. Water pollution is indeed a Murky Monster that is spoiling happy play areas.

Murky Monster is a menacing creature without a spark of good in him. All the fish in the play are blissfully happy until Murky Monster makes his appearance. Then every one of them becomes an exaggerated would-be hero or heroine. Each wants to exhibit his or her bravery and loyalty to the king. When the bay it at last saved from pollution, every fish becomes an ever-grateful citizen. A unity of feeling among the fish (in their loyalty to each other and their concern for the homeland) will make the skit sparkle.

This production can be planned for any location where a water pistol won't be too damaging. A spot in a park or near a campfire would be ideal. Triggerfish must be a reliable person who will shoot his water pistol only on cue.

Costume the fish if you wish and as you wish. Bathing suits would make ideal basic costumes with, for example, crowns for Kingfish, Queenfish, and Sunfish. To make a costume for Murky Monster, use a piece of dark cloth twice as long as the distance from his shoulders to his ankles and about a yard wide.

Fold the cloth in half. In the center of the fold cut a hole large enough for his head. Starting at the bottom, tear the cloth in strips, making long streamers. When Murky Monster swoops about the stage, swinging his arms, he should resemble oil or gunk floating on water.

Characters

KINGFISH	BLOWFISH
QUEENFISH	SAWFISH
SUNFISH	GOLDFISH
MURKY MONSTER	TRIGGERFISH
SWORDFISH	OTHER FISH

SCENE. *An unpolluted bay where fish swim happily.* Kingfish, Queenfish, *and* Sunfish *are downstage center, with other fish standing in a line a little behind them.* Swordfish, Blowfish, Sawfish, Goldfish, *and* Triggerfish *are at the end of the line on the left of the royal fish.* Triggerfish *wears a two-gun holster containing filled water pistols.*

KINGFISH. I am the Kingfish.

QUEENFISH. I am the Queenfish.

SUNFISH. I am Sunfish, their very bright child.

OTHER FISHES (*speaking in chorus*). We are the fish that swim in this unpolluted bay.

ALL FISH (*Singing to tune of* "Turkey in the Straw").

We like to go a-swimming on a bright and sunny day;
We swim and we splash in this unpolluted bay.
With our hands in our pockets
And our pockets in our pants,
Every little fish does a hoochy-koochy dance.

KINGFISH. This is a happy play area.

MURKY MONSTER (*offstage*). Heh! Heh! Heh! That's what you think! (*Enters and swoops around stage menacingly, swinging his arms back and forth.*)

KINGFISH. Who are you?

MURKY MONSTER. I am a murky monster. I've come to pollute your bay. Heh! Heh! Heh!

ALL FISH. No! No! No!

MURKY MONSTER. Yes! Yes! Yes! I've come to stay.

KINGFISH. Oh, who will free our bay of this Murky Monster who has come to pollute our waters?

OTHER FISH. Me! Me! Me!

KINGFISH. One at a time. (Swordfish *steps forward and waves cardboard sword in air.*)

SWORDFISH. I am a swordfish. I shall pierce the Murky Monster. (*He rushes at the monster and puts his sword through the streamers that extend from one arm.*)

MURKY MONSTER (*swooping around stage*). Heh! Heh! Heh! Piercing just stirs me up. (Swordfish *is crushed by his defeat. Slumps and goes behind other fish where he can watch without being noticed.* Blowfish *steps forward.*)

BLOWFISH. I am a blowfish. I shall blow this Murky Monster from our bay. (*Blows as he crosses stage.* Murky Monster *dodges here and there.*)

MURKY MONSTER. Heh! Heh! Heh! Blow me out, and blow me in. I'm here to stay. (Blowfish, *also defeated, slumps and stands near* Swordfish. Sawfish *steps forward holding up cardboard saw.*)

SAWFISH. I am a sawfish. I shall divide him. (*Goes after* Murky Monster *who sidesteps him.*)

MURKY MONSTER. Heh! Heh! Heh! Divide me and you'll have two Murky Monsters. (Sawfish *joins the others in defeat.* Goldfish *steps forward holding up gold-colored cardboard.*)

GOLDFISH. I am a goldfish. I shall tempt him to join me and then drag him to the bottom of the bay. (*Shines gold in front of* Murky Monster *who pays no attention and laughs.*)

MURKY MONSTER. Heh! Heh! Heh! I am not tempted to join with gold. (Goldfish, *defeated, joins other defeated fish.* Triggerfish *steps forward and pulls out one water pistol.*)

TRIGGERFISH. I am a triggerfish. I have a pure-water pistol. I shall—(*points water pistol at* Murky Monster) DILUTE you. (*Shoots water at* Murky Monster, *who clutches breast.*)

MURKY MONSTER. I am diluted. Foiled again! (*Drops to bottom of stage.*)

ALL FISH. Yeah! (Kingfish *and* Queenfish *stand next to* Triggerfish. Sunfish *falls on her knees in front of him. All other fish point to him.*) Our hero!

KINGFISH. Triggerfish, I am proud of you. You have saved our bay from Murky Monster by diluting him. That was a whale of an idea! (Triggerfish *has been holding second water pistol. He now aims it up into the air.*)

TRIGGERFISH. You said it! (*Shoots water up like spout of a whale.*)

KINGFISH. Let's celebrate!

(*All fish sing to the tune of* "Turkey in the Straw.")

Now we'll go a-swimming on a bright and sunny day;
We'll swim and we'll splash in an unpolluted bay.
With our hands in our pockets
And our pockets in our pants,
All the fishes do a hootchy-koochy dance.
Boom-de-de-a-da! Boom! Boom!

LET'S FOOL SOMEONE

Introduction

Half the fun of playing a joke on someone comes in planning it. If the joke backfires there is a big letdown. In this short skit, two friends plan to fool a third friend. The light in their eyes and the tone of their voices show how excited they are. The third friend plays his part deadpan, that is, with no expression on his face. He pretends that he is being fooled until the last line, which he must say loudly and clearly. When the joke backfires, the girls exaggerate their disgust and disappointment.

Read the skit and then imagine that you are in this situation. Use your own names if you wish. Then exaggerate all your reactions.

You can make changes in the script to meet your needs. The characters may be two boys and a girl, two girls and a boy, all girls, or all boys. You can use a scarecrow prop as in the script; or you can substitute another figure: a ghost for Halloween, a Santa for Christmas, a snowman for a winter program, or any other appropriate figure large enough for two to hide behind. If necessary, you can drape a chair, carton, or bush and ask the audience to pretend that it is a scarecrow or whatever figure you have chosen.

If you change the kind of figure, or if you give girls' parts to boys, it will be necessary to change some of the lines of the skit.

Characters

SUSIE BUTLER DUDLEY THOMPSON

LIZZIE TAYLOR

SCENE. *A garden.* Susie Butler *is busy putting finishing touches on a large scarecrow dressed like a woman.* Lizzie Taylor *enters and watches with admiration for a moment.*

LIZZIE. Susie Butler!

SUSIE *(turning).* Well, hello!

LIZZIE. What are you doing, Susie Butler?

SUSIE. I'm making a scarecrow to protect my garden.

LIZZIE. A woman scarecrow?

SUSIE. Why not? (Lizzie *shrugs as if saying,* "I don't know.")

LIZZIE. That's a good idea, Susie. A woman scarecrow can scare crows. And you know what?

SUSIE. What?

LIZZIE. Your woman scarecrow looks real enough to talk.

SUSIE. Do you really think so?

LIZZIE. I really think so, Susie Butler.

SUSIE. Then let's do something!

LIZZIE. What?

SUSIE. Let's fool someone.

LIZZIE. How?

SUSIE. Let's hide behind the scarecrow and fool the next person who comes along.

LIZZIE. How?

SUSIE. I'll talk and make the person think that the scarecrow is talking to him.

LIZZIE. Great! That's a good joke.

SUSIE. Here comes Dudley Thompson. Let's fool him.

(Girls quickly hide behind scarecrow. Dudley *enters.)*

SUSIE *(disguising her voice)*. Hello, little boy.

(Dudley *looks around. Sees no one. He speaks to the scarecrow.*)

DUDLEY. Hello.

SUSIE. What is your name, little boy?

DUDLEY. Dudley Thompson.

SUSIE. Where do you live?

DUDLEY. 318 Charles Street.

SUSIE. Did you ever meet a talking scarecrow before today?

DUDLEY. No.

SUSIE. Isn't it fun to meet a talking scarecrow?

DUDLEY. Yes, it's nice to meet you. Sorry I can't stay. I have to go now.

SUSIE. Goodbye, Dudley Thompson.

DUDLEY. Goodbye, SUSIE BUTLER!

(Dudley *turns and exits as girls emerge from behind scarecrow. They slump in despair, look at each other, and exit.*)

PLAY A PART

SALT IN THE SOUP

Introduction

In this skit the characters are exaggerated "rubes," as stock characters from the farm once were called. They resemble no farm people living or dead.

When Ma calls she sounds like a champion hog caller, making the rafters ring at a fair: "Liz-ZEEEE! Hi-RAAAM! Til-LEEEEE!" Others use a flat tone of voice and lumbering motions.

Ma and the children can be very funny as each watches the salt fall slowly into the soup and then stirs the pot with great satisfaction. Aunt Emma has an excellent opportunity to pantomime the role of a snoopy relative. The confusion at the end of the skit should be terrific but controlled, so that everyone is quiet when Pa belts out the punch line, "Aunt Emma, you need soup!"

In this account of what happened once when far too many people added salt to the soup, there might be any rearrangement of characters to fit a local situation—all boys or all girls. A hilarious production might result from having a boy dressed as Ma or a girl dressed as Pa. An account of this salting-the-soup incident appears in several folk stories. Each version is a bit different so adjust the production to meet your local needs.

To make a stove, paint a picture of the front of an old-fashioned stove on a large packing box. Or place a big pot in the center of a fireplace. For a camp play, put the pot over an unlit campfire. Ma could be sitting on a low stool rather than in a rocking chair. And if a braided rug isn't available, let Ma darn a big pile of socks or mend some bulky material.

Characters

MA	PA
LIZZIE	TILLY
HIRAM	AUNT EMMA

Scene. *Kitchen-living room of a farm shack. Upstage center is an old-fashioned stove on which there rests a large kettle with a big spoon in it. Next to the stove is a small table on which are placed a crock filled with salt, an old-fashioned ladle, and two cups.*

As the scene opens, Ma is sitting in a rocking chair, braiding a rug. Scraps are around her feet. Lizzie, Hiram, *and* Tilly *are seated on aisle seats in the audience.*

MA *(yelling).* Lizzie! (*She says* Liz-ZEEE!) Come put salt in the soup. Aunt Emma's coming to supper.

LIZZIE *(yelling from audience).* Can't I'm washing. You do it.

MA. Can't. I'm braiding. Hiram! (Hi-RAAAM!) Come put salt in the soup. Aunt Emma's coming to supper.

HIRAM (*yelling from audience*). Can't. I'm hoeing. You do it.

MA. Can't. I'm braiding. Tilly! (Til-LEEE!) Come put salt in the soup. Aunt Emma's coming to supper.

TILLY *(yelling from audience).* Can't. I'm feeding chicks. You do it.

MA *(getting up with great effort).* Guess I better put salt in the soup. Aunt Emma's coming to supper. *(She picks up a handful of salt and stands so that the audience can see it falling into the kettle. She stirs soup. Exits right. Lizzie enters left.)*

LIZZIE. Guess I better put salt in the soup. Aunt Emma's

coming for supper. *(She picks up a handful of salt and turns so that the audience can see it falling into the kettle. Exits left.* Hiram *enters right.)*

HIRAM. Guess I better put salt in the soup. Aunt Emma's coming to supper. *(Picks up handful of salt and stands so that the audience can see it falling into the kettle. Exits right.* Tilly *enters left.)*

TILLY. Guess I better put salt in the soup. Aunt Emma's coming to supper. *(Picks up handful of salt. Stands so that audience can see it falling into the kettle. Exits right.* Aunt Emma *enters left.)*

AUNT EMMA (*yelling*). Hello! Hello! Ezra! Marty! Lizzie! Hiram! Tilly! Hello! Hmmmm. Nobody indoors. Guess I'll make myself to home. *(She puts down her bag. Takes off her hat. Looks around the house. Inspects the braided rug and shrugs as if she doesn't think much of it. Sniffs the air.)* Hmmmm. Smells like soup. I do like soup. *(Goes to stove.)* It is soup! Bet this soup needs salt. *(She adds a handful, and stirs the soup.)* Might as well have a little before the folks come in. *(She dips ladle into pot and puts soup in cup. Comes front stage and starts to drink one pretend swallow. She throws the cup down and begins to choke.)*

AUNT EMMA *(making queer sound as she holds throat).* A-eh-aeh-a-eh-a-eh!

MA, LIZZIE, HIRAM, TILLY *(rushing in).* Aunt Emma! Aunt Emma! What's wrong?

PA *(entering left).* What's wrong?

LIZZIE (*imitating* Aunt Emma). Aunt Emma! She's going a-eh-a-a-eh. (*Confusion continues.*)

PA *(loudly).* Wait a minute! Wait a minute! Quiet! (Aunt Emma *continues to choke quietly and others are still.)* I know what to do. (Pa *goes to stove. Dips soup into remaining cup. Comes to* Aunt Emma.) Aunt Emma, you need soup!

(Aunt Emma *makes one last big noise and collapses with a grand gesture.*)

OR MAKE POT HOLDERS

Introduction

Emily has thought of a way to get around the problem of being asked to do the same things over and over each year at camp. She is a determined young person as she sets about deliberately to carry out her plan. She is not rude to her mother, but she pays little attention to what Mother is saying.

Mother is interested in what Emily is doing. Although she is curious about Emily's actions, she hesitates to ask her why she is piling an odd assortment of things on the table.

In the first part of this skit the atmosphere is more important than the actual lines. Emily must move quickly in piling the things on the table, but if she cannot complete her stage business before Mother has finished her lines, then Mother must continue to talk, making up lines as she goes along. Emily may cut Mother short on all lines except those related to pot holders. The audience must know that even Mother, patient and understanding as she is, has had enough of pot holders and their making.

Characters in the skit need not be a mother and daughter. They may be father and son, mother and son, or father and daughter. Furnish the room as you wish, but avoid spending undue work on the stage and the settings. At least one table will be needed with space near it for overflow of the collections and pot holders.

Mother could be sweeping with a broom or carpet sweeper rather than dusting. Or, if the skit is given out of doors, Mother could be working with a trowel or lawn clippers. Articles could be piled on a picnic or card table or make pot holders.

Characters

Emily Mother

Scene. *Living room. Furnishings include a chair, left, bookcase, chest of drawers, and small table, center front. A piece of paper and pencil is placed on table. As scene opens,* Mother *is dusting the chair.* Emily *enters right, carrying a box which she sets on table.*

EMILY. Well, there's the insect collection that I made at camp last year. (Emily *checks off item on the paper as* Mother *stops dusting, crosses to table, and admires collection.*)

MOTHER. Emily, you did a wonderful job at camp, making that insect collection. Now that it's spring you can collect more insects, here at home.

EMILY. Where are the leaves I pressed at camp last summer?

MOTHER. On the bottom shelf of the bookcase. (Emily *gets large loose-leaf notebook. Places it on table and checks list as* Mother *continues to talk.)*

MOTHER. That's another good idea, Emily. You can collect and press leaves here at home, right now. You can see the difference between the new leaves in our yard and the mature leaves you found at camp.

EMILY. Where are the pine cones I collected at camp?

MOTHER. They are still in that big bag in the closet. (Emily *exits and re-enters quickly with bag which she places on pile and checks list as* Mother *continues to talk.*) Emily, I don't understand what you are doing? Are you going to make Christmas decorations early this year? This early? I'm sorry we couldn't use the pine cones last year.

EMILY. Where are the pot holders I made at camp last year?

MOTHER. In the top drawer of the chest. (Emily *gets them.*) Just as good as new. (Emily *adds them to the pile and checks her list as* Mother *continues to talk.*)

MOTHER. They are new, Emily. I'm sorry. Let's face it. I'll never be able to use all the pot holders you have made in kindergarten, on the playground, at Brownie troop meetings, and then at camp last year. There is a limit. Now maybe your grandmother—

EMILY *(interrupting).* I know. Now, I guess that's it. Where is my duffle bag?

MOTHER. Duffle bag? Why do you want your duffle bag now?

EMILY. I'm packing for camp.

MOTHER. Packing for camp? Insect collection, leaves, pine cones, pot holders. These are the things you brought home from camp last year.

EMILY. I know. I am taking my collections, and my pot holders back to camp.

MOTHER. Why?

EMILY. When I get to camp, I'll have my collections and my pot holders. This year I won't have to collect insects, mount leaves, pick up pine cones, or MAKE POT HOLDERS! This year, I'll do something new!

MOTHER. Emily!

ROCK THE BABY, GRANNY

Introduction

Here is a skit where the fun lies in controlled confusion. Every player must cooperate in "whooping it up," and then being quiet at exactly the right time. You can substitute the latest dance craze for rock 'n' roll. Or you can make up a new dance of your own and call it "Rock the baby, partner, but don't you rock too hard."

"Rock the Baby, Granny" gives excellent opportunities for pantomime, that wonderful art of telling a story without words, telling it only by bodily movement and facial expression. Before you learn and practice lines, practice the pantomime—the pretense—of looking for things, picking some up, laying some down, putting some in a bag or purse. Show your moods by the way you talk and stand.

As in all skits, the characters are exaggerated. Mr. Stewart, a businessman, speaks seriously and firmly to his son as he gives him advice. And then Mr. Stewart nearly goes crazy from the racket! Mrs. Stewart, a fussy housewife, seems out of her mind as she hurries to get out of the house. Granny is more like a great-grandmother in the way she dresses, walks, and talks. Kenny is completely bored with life, and Mary Jo is very, very sweet.

If you prefer, you can have a cast with all the friends played by boys, or all by girls. Even with a mixed cast there is no need to have an even number of each. There could be as few as three extra friends, or as many as can be fitted onto the stage.

Timing is all important in this skit. Don't allow the music to be played too long. End with a lot of zip!

Characters

KENNY STEWART	GRANNY
MR. STEWART	MARY JO
MRS. STEWART	OTHER BOYS AND GIRLS

SCENE. *Living room of the Stewart home. A record player is placed upstage center; a small table downstage center; armchair with end table next to it right center front; desk or chest with drawers left back. There may be an extra chair or two to make the room look comfortable; but the center of the floor must be left fairly clear for dancing.*

There are two entrances: left front, leading to other parts of the upstage house and right, leading to the street.

As the scene opens, Mr. Stewart *is sitting in the armchair reading a newspaper.* Kenny *enters, carrying a zippered bag into which he is stuffing a bag of cookies. He picks up a small bank, shakes out the coins and puts them in his pocket, picks up other things, puts some down, puts some into his bag or into his pockets.* Mr. Stewart *watches him for a few minutes before speaking.)*

MR. STEWART. Kenny, what are you doing?

KENNY. I'm leaving home.

MR. STEWART. Leaving home? Why?

KENNY. Nothing to do here.

MR. STEWART. Nothing to do here?

KENNY. Well, nothing new. Same old things. *(Turns to look for more things.)*

MR. STEWART *(firmly)*. Ken, look at me. (Ken *turns and faces his father.*) Ken, there is plenty to do here, but you are in a rut.

KENNY. Rut? I'll say I'm in a rut!

MR. STEWART *(slowly)*. What you need is a new interest, a new interest here at home.

KENNY. What new interest?

MR. STEWART. That's for you to find out. *(Picks up paper as doorbell rings.)*

KENNY (*going to door*). Hi, Mary Jo! Come in.

MR. STEWART *(rising)*. Hello, Mary Jo.

MARY JO *(coming downstage)*. Oh, don't get up, Mr. Stewart. Kenny, I have to show you something. *(She places package she is carrying on small table.)*

KENNY. What now, Mary Jo?

MARY JO (*opening package*). I'll show you.

KENNY. Mary Jo, you know I don't like music.

MARY JO. But Kenny, these are super! *(He won't look.)* Kenny Stewart, you are in the dumps. Do you know what's wrong with you? *(He faces her.)* You are in a rut. You need a new interest. (Mr. Stewart *lowers paper.*)

KENNY. What did you say?

MARY JO. You are in a rut. You need a new interest. (Kenny *throws up his hands. Crosses back of his father's chair.*)

MR. STEWART. Excuse me. *(Exits.)*

MARY JO. What's wrong? What did I say?

KENNY (*coming forward*). Nothing new. (*Sits in armchair. Leans forward, as if thinking.)* Well, maybe you're right. Everyone else likes rock 'n' roll. I might like it. Play your records, Mary Jo.

MARY JO. Oh, good. Let's get the other kids. May I phone?

KENNY. Go right ahead. (*Bell rings.*) Someone's at the door. *(She starts to phone as he ushers in other boys and girls.)*

MARY JO. Susie, come right over to Kenny's. Tell everyone to come. *(There is much greeting as group comes in. They rush in breathlessly during the next few moments as play goes on.)*

MARY JO. Now listen to this. *(Holds up record.)* With this one we ought to try "Rock the Baby." Rock the Baby, Kenny, but don't you rock too hard. *(She hands the record to one of the boys who puts it on the player.)* Now, Ken. Get the beat. (*All start to dance and yell in time to music.* Kenny *is reluctant at first, but is soon dancing with everyone else. During the confusion Mr. Stewart enters with his attaché case. He picks up pencil, papers, and so on. Kenny motions for music to stop.)*

KENNY. Dad, where are you going?

MR. STEWART. To the office.

KENNY. To the office? On Saturday? (Mr. Stewart *nods.*) Dad, you are in a rut! You need a new interest, an interest at home.

MR. STEWART. Go on with your new interest, Ken. It's too much for me. (*Exits.*)

(*Boys and girls start to dance again.* Mrs. Stewart *enters, puts on hat, picks up this and that and puts them in her purse.* Kenny *stops music.*)

KENNY. Mom, what's the matter?

MRS. STEWART. I'm going shopping.

KENNY. But Mom, you went shopping this morning. (*She nods.*) Mom, you are in a rut! You need a new interest, an interest at home.

MRS. STEWART. Go on with your interest, Kenny. It's too much for me. (*She exits. Music starts again.* Granny *enters. She watches one couple and then another.* Kenny *stops music.*)

KENNY. Granny, are you leaving, too? Are you going back to Oshkosh?

GRANNY. Leaving? Going back to Oshkosh?

MARY JO. Please stay, Granny. You see we all came here because we wanted Kenny to have a new interest.

GRANNY. A new interest?

KENNY. Yes, Granny. I have a new interest—rock 'n' roll.

GRANNY. So that's it. Rock 'n' roll. Well, I have a new interest, too. Rock 'n' roll. On with the dance!

KENNY. Be my partner, Granny. (*They take center front positions.*) Now, rock the baby Granny, but don't rock too hard!

(*Everyone starts to dance as curtain is lowered.*)

OPERATION SATELLITE

Introduction

The great fun in this skit lies in making a ridiculous situation seem serious. And to make it seem completely serious, every witch and every wizard must act as if the Grand Wizard is the wisest creature that ever existed. Each player must follow the Grand Wizard's every word with rapt attention and concern. Each must rejoice when Slowcum announces her clever solution to the modern problem.

The incantations, the spoken charms or spells, must be solemn, the words spoken with great feeling. After all, witches and wizards understand the power of incantations and depend on them to get the results they want.

Characters

GRAND WIZARD	OLDROT
SLOWCUM	HOOTNICK
HATTRAP	WITCHES AND WIZARDS

Scene. *Meeting place of witches and wizards.* Grand Wizard *stands behind a big black pot, placed center stage.* Hattrap *sits on a carton to the right of the pot, stirring something in it. Oldrot sits on a box left of the pot.* Hootnick *stands near* Grand Wizard. *Other witches and wizards are grouped around the main characters in such a way as to allow* Grand Wizard *to move freely around front stage.*

As the curtain rises, wizards and witches are ready to chant a spell. If there is no curtain, all except Slowcum *enter mouthing,* "Where is Slowcum?" *and take positions. At signal from* Grand Wizard *they chant.*

Witches and Wizards. Hicketty, hicketty, hoecum!
Blicketty, blicketty, blowcum!
Ziss-boom! Ziss-boom!
Come back, Slowcum!

Grand Wizard. Where is Slowcum? Every witch and every wizard is here except Slowcum.

Hattrap. Try it again, sir. You need a strong chant to bring back Slowcum.

Grand Wizard. Why do we need a strong chant to bring back Old Witch Slowcum?

Hattrap. Because, sir, Old Witch Slowcum has young ideas,

Grand Wizard. Young ideas? Whoever heard of a witch with young ideas?

(*Other witches and wizards look at each other, shake heads, gesture, and mouth,* "I don't know. I don't know. Not me. Not me.")

Grand Wizard (*to* Hattrap). Do you know what young idea Witch Slowcum is trying?

Hattrap. Yes, sir. Slowcum broke her broom.

Grand Wizard. I know, I know. The nincompoop broke her broom. Then she came to me—to me, the Grand Wizard—and asked, "What shall I do?"

Hattrap. And you said?

GRAND WIZARD. I said, "Don't bother me. Go fly a kite!"

HATTRAP. And so—?

GRAND WIZARD. So what?

HATTRAP. Slowcum is doing what you told her to do.

GRAND WIZARD. What I told her to do?

HATTRAP. Yes, sir. You said, "Go fly a kite." Slowcum is flying through the air on a kite.

GRAND WIZARD. Oh, no! Slowcum flying through the air on a kite? "Go fly a kite" is just an expression.

HATTRAP. To a witch, sir, flying a kite is a means of travel.

GRAND WIZARD (*pacing floor, wringing hands*). Oh, no! Not Slowcum on a kite! Not tonight. (*Other witches and wizards are wringing hands, shaking heads.*) For tonight (*Pauses and faces front.*)

The wind will roar.
The rain will pour.
Old men will snore.

Well, anyway. All together. Let's try again. Let's bring back Slowcum. Ready?

WITCHES AND WIZARDS. Hicketty, hicketty, hoecum!
Blicketty, blicketty, blowcum!
Ziss-boom! Ziss-boom!
Come back, Slowcum!

(*Sounds of great storm offstage. If no wind machine is available, pound drums or tin pans to make loud noise. In slides* Slowcum, *hat smashed in, clothes torn, dragging torn kite.*)

WITCHES AND WIZARDS (*gathering around* Slowcum). Are you all right? Are you all right? What happened?

GRAND WIZARD (*raising arms*). Give her air. Give her air. (*One witch picks up bellows and blows air on* Slowcum. Grand Wizard, *disgusted, shooes her away and motions for others to spread out.*)

GRAND WIZARD (*hands on hips, glowering at* Slowcum). All right, Slowcum, what happened?

SLOWCUM (*meekly*). I took your suggestion, sir. I flew on a kite.

GRAND WIZARD. My suggestion? "Go fly a kite?" That's just an expression.

SLOWCUM. Yes, sir, I know; but it's a good suggestion, too. Flying on a kite was glorious, wonderful, exotic, stimulating, until—

GRAND WIZARD. Until what? Slowcum, I bet you got off course. Why must you get off course? Will you never learn to ride on course?

SLOWCUM. No, sir. I mean, yes, sir. This time I was on course, my very own course, and so was a satellite. I bumped into a satellite.

WIZARD (*alarmed*). A satellite! That's dangerous. A satellite on your course. It could be on my course. Or (*pointing to other witches and wizards*) your course, or your course, or your course. What shall we do?

WITCHES AND WIZARDS (*pointing to themselves and each other*). Yes, yes, yes.

GRAND WIZARD. What shall we do?

OLDROT. I know. Let's do what mortals do.

GRAND WIZARD. What's that?

OLDROT. Picket.

WITCHES AND WIZARDS. Good idea. Good idea. (*All except* Slowcum *and* Grand Wizard *get in line and circle about saying,*) Down with Satellites. Down with Satellites. (Slowcum *sits bewildered, shaking her head.*)

GRAND WIZARD (*lifting his hands*). Quiet! (*Others stand still.*) Well, Slowcum.

SLOWCUM. Do you really want satellites to come down, down on our hovels, down on our snakes, down on our frogs and our bogs, down on everything we hold near and dear?

OTHERS. No, no, no.

GRAND WIZARD. What then?

HOOTNICK. I know. We'll petition. (*Makes sweeping gesture.*)

All the witches and the wizards of the world will sign a petition. (*Walks across stage pretending to unroll a long petition.*) Miles and miles of petition, We'll send it to our congressmen. We'll say, "We won't vote for you unless you abolish satellites."

SLOWCUM. Do witches vote?

OTHERS (*shaking heads*). No, no, no.

GRAND WIZARD. Think! Think! Think! Everybody think! (Witches and Wizards *put hands on foreheads, close eyes, screw up faces.*)

SLOWCUM. I know. As the mortals say, "If you can't fight 'em, join 'em."

GRAND WIZARD. What? Join the mortals?

SLOWCUM. No, join the satellites. Let's ride the satellites.

WITCHES AND WIZARDS. Yes! Yes! Sounds like fun. Ride the satellites.

GRAND WIZARD (*raising hands*). Quiet! Let me think. Witches and wizards riding satellites. That's not customary.

OLDROT. No, sir. But it sounds like fun.

SLOWCUM. And I've thought of a new incantation.

Away with brooms!
Away with kites!
Witches ride
The satellites! Zoom!

GRAND WIZARD. That's good! We'll do it! We shall inaugurate "Operation Satellite." We'll give the official incantation. Ready? All together.

WITCHES AND WIZARDS. Away with brooms!

Away with kites!
Witches ride
The satellites! Zoom!

(*If there is no curtain,* Witches and Wizards *form a snake chain, that is, they line up behind* Grand Wizard. *Each places his backstage hand on the shoulder of the person in front of him. Exit saying incantation,* "Away with brooms!" *etc.*)

PLAYLETS AND DRAMATIC SCENES

Playlets and dramatic scenes are short and often incomplete. They are not constructed as plays are with an introduction, a body, and a climax. Before the curtain rises on some scenes, a narrator explains to the audience what has happened, what incident or event is involved. In a play characters would be obliged to give this information. As the curtain closes on some playlets or dramatic scenes, the audience is left wondering "What happened next?" A play would have a conclusion. In some playlets a narrator tells the entire story while players pantomime the action. It is possible to pantomime a full-length play, but it is not practical except in ballet, where the main interest is in the dancing. Some playlets are complete in themselves; but because they are short, the plot is uncomplicated. Unlike a play, playlets have little interaction of events.

Don't underestimate the value of putting on a playlet or a dramatic scene because you consider it to be too simple for your age or too short for a performance. A short dramatic piece offers an actor a chance to give a sustained performance for a brief period. Each character is an individual person involved in a specific problem. He is more than a type. The audience must sense his personality at once. Each character must work with the entire cast to bring the scene quickly to a high point.

Some playlets and dramatic scenes offer excellent opportunity for pantomime, an art essential for every actor. In pantomime every movement must be meaningful. Every facial expression, every gesture, every movement of the entire body must help to create a stage picture and a mood for the production.

Pantomime is done in different kinds of situation. An actor may pantomime on a silent stage. Or he may pantomime the lines, or spoken words, of another actor. As in some of the playlets given here, an actor may be called upon to pantomime while a narrator tells a story or part of a story, or while music is being played. This type of pantomime requires perfect timing.

A narrator needs a great deal of practice in either speaking or reading his lines. He must memorize his part, or know it so well that he can recite most of it without lowering his head, only occasionally glancing at the page at the end of a paragraph. The head-up stance is important because the narrator must project his voice to the back of the room without straining his vocal chords. He must breathe correctly and know when to pause and take a deep breath in order to be able to finish a sentence without loss of volume.

To avoid monotony, a narrator must vary the pace of his speech, saying some phrases more quickly than others. He must change the pitch of his voice effectively. In short, he must follow the general rules for good public speaking.

Some groups may wish to use more than one narrator when the narration is fairly long. Each voice has its own pitch and tone, and thus adds variety to a production.

Playlets and dramatic scenes fit well into many types of programs, such as entertainment after a dinner or an award meeting;

as part of a longer program that might include music and recitations or choral speaking; as part of a club meeting; or as a classroom presentation. A full-length program might consist of two or three playlets and dramatic scenes, or a combination of a skit, a puppet play, and a dramatic scene, or any other combination of dramatic material.

WHY THE NIGHTINGALE SINGS GLORIOUSLY

Introduction

You can pantomime a dramatic scene and let the audience guess what the story is about; or, you can pantomime while a narrator tells the story. For *Why the Nightingale Sings Gloriously* you can have one narrator or two, with one telling the legend and one telling the story.

To make the dramatic scene effective the voices of the narrators and the pantomime of the actors must be perfectly timed. The narrator should tell the story, not read it, although he may glance at the book now and then if he wishes. The actors must listen carefully as they pantomime. Their actions must not get ahead of the story. The production, short as it is, must be smooth.

Although the scene is brief, Mary and Joseph must express a variety of emotions: weariness, alarm, fear, anger, relief, gratitude, and contentment. What emotions do the robbers feel? Happiness? At one point, yes, when they think they have caught Mary and Joseph unprotected. Greed? Fear? These and many other emotions you will think of yourself.

Scenery is unnecessary. However, if an untrimmed tree stands on the stage, Mary and Joseph may rest beside it. Or, if you wish, you can make a large "stone" by tying crushed newspaper around a cardboard carton and covering the top and sides with papier-mache. Mary and Joseph may rest beside the stone.

A bird is unnecessary. Mary and Joseph look up when it is heard (offstage). The first sound of the bird should be raucous, shrill and ugly, and not like any real bird. At the end of the scene, if you have a bird whistle or a bird record, play the song of a thrush.

Mary carries a baby doll, wrapped in a blanket. Joseph carries a heavy walking stick and a cloth bundle in which the gifts from the wise men are supposedly wrapped.

Characters

FIRST NARRATOR — JOSEPH
SECOND NARRATOR — ROBBERS
MARY

(*Throughout the performance* Mary *and* Joseph *and the* Robbers *pantomime the actions and the emotions indicated by the* Second Narrator, *the storyteller. The thrush screeches or sings—offstage—on cue.*)

FIRST NARRATOR. Did you ever hear
the song of a nightingale?
A kind of thrush
that sings at night?
Some people say
that of all the birds that sing
the thrush's voice
is the most glorious.
Legend says
that once upon a time
the thrush had a shrill, ugly voice,

a screeching sound
worse than the call of a crow.
Something happened long ago
to change his song.

Second Narrator. When Mary and Joseph left Bethlehem and fled with the baby Jesus to Egypt, they took with them three costly gifts that the wise men had left—gold, frankincense, and myrrh. The distance from Bethlehem to Egypt was at least four hundred miles, and as day after day passed, Mary and Joseph became very tired. Their steps grew shorter. They could hardly lift their feet. At last they sank wearily to the ground. Joseph placed beside him his stout walking stick and the bundle of precious gifts.

Mary cuddled the baby Jesus for a few moments and then, placing her head on Joseph's shoulder, fell asleep. Very soon Joseph, too, was nodding, even as he sat in an upright position. The moon rose high in the sky, and all was still.

In the stillness there came robbers who knew about the costly gifts that Joseph carried. They had followed the little family all the way from Bethlehem, waiting for a chance to steal the gifts of the kings. At last, when Mary and Joseph and the Babe were all alone and unprotected, the robbers crept closer and closer.

For some reason unknown to him, a little thrush had failed to sleep that night. Perhaps he sensed danger as he watched the robbers approach. With a loud and raucous voice he called out, "Ehhhhhhh! Ehhhhhhh! Ehhhhhh!"

Mary awoke with a start, clutching the baby Jesus to her breast. Joseph grabbed his walking stick, jumped to his feet, and chased the robbers from the scene.

The little bird, again for some reason unknown to him, began to sing—not in that raucous voice, but in sweet-sounding trills and ripples like a flute. On and on he sang. Mary and Joseph listened with amazement.

At last when they were rested, Mary and Joseph arose with the baby Jesus and continued on their journey to Egypt.

FIRST NARRATOR. What about the bird?
Legend says he is
a special kind of thrush,
a nightingale,
which still sings gloriously in the dark
in memory of the night
when he saved the Holy Family,
Mary, Joseph, and the baby Jesus.

THE SUMMER MAKER

Introduction

Indians and fur-covered animals pantomime the action of this Chippewa Indian legend as an *iagoo,* or Chippewa storyteller, relates the tale.

Include as many Indians and animals as practical. The Indians must appear to be constantly cold, until the sun shines. Before you practice the playlet as a whole, let everyone pretend that he is very cold; then pretend that he is getting gradually warmer.

The animals may walk on all fours, or they may walk on their hind legs, slumped over in a characteristic pose. As in other Indian legends, the animals are something like human beings. In this playlet they point to themselves and make other gestures as they brag. They may do acrobatic tricks as they frisk about in the cold, but the tricks must not delay the playlet.

You and the audience may simply imagine that there is a cloud hiding the sun, or you can construct a paper canopy, tacked at its four corners to sticks or poles. Four actors, representing the four corners of the earth, may hold the cloud above the actors. When the wolverine is ready for his third attempt to break the cloud, actors lower the canopy to be sure that the wolverine can crash through the paper and rip it to pieces.

If you use a cloud you must use a sun also. A cardboard sun can be suspended from the ceiling above the cloud; or it can be nailed to a long pole and held above the cloud.

Characters

IAGOO, or Chippewa storyteller
INDIANS (*as many as practical*)
BEAR
HARE
OTTER
WOLVERINE
OTHER ANIMALS (*if desired*)
MANITOU, messenger from the Great Spirit

SCENE. *The country around Lake Superior many years ago. An iagoo, or storyteller, appears front stage and to one side.*

IAGOO. I, an iagoo, a Chippewa storyteller, will tell you the legend of the summer maker. Many thousands of years ago winter lasted all the year. A great cloud covered the earth so that the sun never shone. The earth was always cold.

The Indians suffered greatly. (Indians *enter rubbing their bodies. They huddle together, trying to keep warm.*) They feared that they would die of the cold.

Only the fur-covered animals enjoyed the cold that lasted all year long, year after year. The fur on their bodies kept them warm.

(*The animals enter one by one and pantomime their fun in the cold.*)

IAGOO. The bear lumbered through the snowbanks.
The hare hopped across the fields.
The otter slid on the ice.
The wolverine jumped with joy high into the air.

Sometimes the animals frisked together as the freezing Indians prayed to the manitous, the spirits. (Indians *raise hands in prayer.*)

"Please," prayed the Indians, "bring us warmth."

At last the Great Spirit heard their prayers and sent a manitou to earth. (*Enter* Manitou.)

Manitou invited the animals to gather around him. (*Animals sit around* Manitou.) The Indians crept slowly from their wigwams to hear what Manitou had to say. (Indians *join the circle of animals.*)

"Oh, clever animals," asked Manitou, "who is the greatest among you?" (*Each animal in turn points to himself as the iagoo continues to tell the story.*)

"I," said the bear. "I am the strongest."

"I," said the hare. "I am the swiftest."

"I," said the otter. "I am the most slippery."

"I," said the wolverine. "I am the most persistent. I never give up."

"Strong, swift, slippery, persistent," said Manitou. "Do you see that cloud? Now, who can jump high enough to make a hole in the cloud?" (*As the iagoo describes the animals' responses to the question, each animal pantomimes a jump.*)

"I," said the bear. He jumped and fell.

"I," said the hare. His jump was wide but not high.

"I," said the otter, but he slid before he could start to jump.

"I," said the wolverine. Now the wolverine jumped once and fell back. He jumped again and almost touched the cloud. He jumped a third time. And he jumped so high that he made a hole in the cloud. The sun shone through. Summer came to earth.

(*Pantomime what you think happened next. What do you think the animals did as the sun made the earth warmer and warmer and fur coats made the animals hotter and hotter? Would they pant and run off to a watering hole?*

What about the Indians? *As they gradually grew warm, perhaps they lifted their hands to welcome the sun and to praise the Great Spirit, who had sent a manitou. No doubt they danced around* Manitou, *thanking him for bringing summer. At the end of the pantomime the iagoo speaks again.*)

IAGOO. And that is how summer came to the earth.

—*The Summer Maker* is based on
an old Chippewa Indian legend.

WHY THE OWL IS SACRED IN HAWAII

Introduction

Long ago in Hawaii an individual could choose anything to be a god for himself and his family. According to legend, an owl agreed to be the god and protector of a common man named Kapoi. Trouble arose when the owl commanded Kapoi to build a temple, because only a chief could build a temple.

The struggle between the owls and the men in this legend gives actors an opportunity to be fighting while keeping the situation on stage under control. The owls must swoop around fiercely as the humans cringe in fear of them. Everything must suddenly grow quiet when Big Owl gives the signal.

Use as many owls and chief's men as as practical. If you wish to have fewer players than listed in the play, let the chief appear with only one or two of his men.

Do not use masks that cover the face. Owls must be able to see what they are doing, and Big Owl must be heard. You may use half-face masks. Enlarge the holes for eyes. Paint white circles around them. Staple paper owl ears in place on the masks.

PLAY A PART

Characters

STORYTELLER — CHIEF'S MEN
CRIER — HIGH CHIEF
KAPOI — OTHER OWLS
BIG OWL

SCENE. *The island of Oahu, Hawaii. A few sticks for making a fire and a few flat stones are placed downstage center. Farther back to the left side of the stage is a nest made of tufts of grass. The nest contains seven pullet-size eggs, as round as possible. (Use shells from which the yolks and whites have been carefully blown.)* Crier *steps forward.*

CRIER. Listen to the tale of your fathers. Learn why the owl is sacred in Hawaii. Remember the promise of Kapoi. "I shall never rob the nest of a bird unless I need eggs for food. Even when hungry I shall leave at least two eggs in each nest so that young birds may hatch." (Cries *goes backstage where he stands.* Storyteller *advances to frontstage, right.*)

STORYTELLER. Long ago on the island of Oahu, near the site where the city of Honolulu now stands, there lived a common man named Kapoi. (Kapoi *enters, carrying a small wooden bowl or woven basket.*) He was a happy man. When Kapoi could not fish, he roamed the hills looking for birds' eggs for his supper. (Kapoi *walks slowly around the stage. Stops when he discovers the bird's nest with eggs.*)

One day Kapoi was very lucky. He found seven owl eggs. (Kapoi *puts eggs in his basket. He comes downstage, puts basket on ground, picks up sticks and holds them in position to start a fire by rubbing the sticks together.*) He started to build a fire in order to cook the eggs for supper, but, before he could rub two sticks together, something happened. (Storyteller *steps backstage as* Big Owl *enters to stand near* Kapoi. Chief's Men *enter and stand in background listening.*)

BIG OWL. Kapoi! Kapoi! Give me back my eggs.

KAPOI. I gathered these eggs. They are mine. I am going to wrap them in ti leaves and cook them for my supper.

BIG OWL. Please give me my eggs. If you take my eggs, there will be no baby birds. What would Hawaii be like without birds?

KAPOI. Hawaii without birds? Oh, no! (*He pauses for a moment as if thinking.*) You are right. If men take your eggs, there will be no baby birds. I'll return your eggs. (*Picks up eggs.*) I'll try again to fish. (*Returns eggs to nest as* Owl *hovers over him.*)

BIG OWL. Thank you! Thank you! (Owl *returns to site of the stones.* Kapoi *returns to center stage.*) Now, Kapoi, I shall be your family god and protector. Build a temple on this spot, Kapoi. (Chief's Men *run offstage.*)

KAPOI. Build a temple? I am a common man. Only a chief can build a temple.

OWL (*commanding*). Build a temple. You have done a great thing. You returned eggs to the nest. There will be young birds on the island. I am now your family god. Build a temple!

KAPOI. I follow your command. (*Kneels to pick up stones.*)

(Chief *followed by his men rushes in.*)

CHIEF. What is the meaning of this? (Kapoi *rises and bows.*)

KAPOI. Big Owl commanded me to build a temple. (*Kneels.*)

CHIEF. You, Kapoi, a common man, build a temple? Only a chief may build a temple. (*To* Chief's Men.) Seize him! Kill him!

(Big Owl *stands between* Chief *and* Kapoi. Big Owl *screams!*)

BIG OWL. Ow-w-wls! Ow-w-wls! Ow-w-wls! (*To the men.*) You shall not kill Kapoi. He saved our eggs. (Owls *appear from everywhere. With slapping wings they beat the* Chief's Men. Big Owl *continues to stand above* Kapoi *and continues to call* "Ow-w-wls!" *At last all the men are on their knees, including the* Chief. Big Owl *stops calling, and all is quiet.*)

CHIEF. Forgive me. Forgive me.

BIG OWL. Rise. (*All rise.*)

CHIEF. Forgive me, Kapoi. (Kapoi *kneels before* Chief. Chief *places his right hand on* Kapoi's *head in blessing.*) The owls are right. They have fought for a great idea. From this day forth owls shall be sacred in Hawaii. (Chief's Men *bow to owls, who return the bow.*) Rise, Kapoi. Behold your family god.

KAPOI (*to* Big Owl). Oh, Sacred Owl, I make a promise. I shall never rob a bird's nest unless I need eggs for food. Even when hungry I shall leave at least two eggs in each nest so that young birds may hatch.

CHIEF. Kapoi, if each man follows your promise, we shall always have birds in Hawaii. (Chief *bows and exits, followed by his men.* Big Owl *goes to nest to protect eggs.* Kapoi *kneels before* Big Owl. Other Owls *hover in background.*)

STORYTELLER. Thank you for listening. May we long remember

Kapoi's promise: "I shall never rob a bird's nest unless I need eggs for food. Even when hungry I shall leave at least two eggs in each nest to allow young birds to hatch." In this way we shall always have birds in our land.

—*Why the Owl Is Sacred in Hawaii*
is based on an old Hawaiian legend.

PIRATES

Introduction

If possible, read Robert Louis Stevenson's *Treasure Island* before producing this scene, a dramatization of Chapter 11, "What I Heard in the Apple Barrel." Discover for yourself that Long John Silver was a good actor as well as a ruthless pirate. Try to understand how Jim Hawkins, an innocent lad away from home, must have felt when he accidentally discovered the fact that members of the crew were pirates.

In dramatizing this scene it was necessary to invent dialogue in some places and simplify it in others. It was necessary also to find some way to set the mood of the scene and let the audience know what thoughts may have been running through Jim's mind. So, Jim talks to a cat, a cat that he might have brought from home. Do not hurry this opening scene.

Long John Silver's lines must be carefully paced. At times he is coaxing the young sailor Dick into becoming what Silver calls "a gentleman of fortune." At other times, Silver reveals himself as the bloodthirsty pirate he really is.

You can produce this scene with costumes and an authentic set, including a barrel, or you can produce it without any properties. Jim can pantomime climbing into a barrel and crouching inside.

PLAY A PART

Characters

NARRATOR	ISRAEL HANDS, a sailor
JIM HAWKINS, a boy	DICK, a sailor
LONG JOHN SILVER, a cook	LOOKOUT (*offstage*)

SCENE. *Deck of a ship. A barrel stands downstage right. Place a small box near the barrel to make it easy for Jim to climb into it. As the scene opens,* Jim *enters carrying a cat. He paces the deck, stopping every few minutes to talk to the cat. He simply pantomimes the talk until the* Narrator *has finished his speech.*)

NARRATOR. Today we present a scene from *Treasure Island* by Robert Louis Stevenson. The good ship, *Hispanola,* is sailing from England under sealed orders to a distant South Sea island.

At the very start of the voyage it was thought that the destination and purpose of the expedition were known to only three persons—Squire Trelawney, Dr. Livesey, and Jim Hawkins, a lad who had found a mysterious map in an old sea chest.

Recorded on this mysterious map was the latitude and longitude of an island and directions for finding a buried treasure, accumulated and left there by Captain Flint, a notorious pirate.

A few weeks after leaving port Mr. Smollett, captain of the ship, learned the purpose of the voyage from the crew. From the beginning he had distrusted this crew, which had been assembled by a one-legged cook named Long John Silver.

Although the captain fears the crew is composed of thieves, the doctor, the squire, and Jim think the captain is wrong. They believe the crew to be an interesting lot of seafaring men. They suspect no wrong until one night when Jim accidentally falls asleep in an apple barrel that the captain had kindly left on deck.

(Jim *now talks aloud to his cat, loud enough that the audience is able to hear every word.*)

JIM. Well, little cat, how do you like seeing the world? Isn't it peaceful here on deck? It's not like old England. Not like the inn my father kept. But one thing's the same for you. You always stay close to the cook.

Speaking of the cook, I'm hungry. Now, how about an apple from the barrel the captain put on deck? Do you want an apple? Well, I do. (*Looks in barrel.*) The barrel's almost empty. We'll have to climb into it if we want an apple. (Jim, *still holding the cat, climbs into the barrel. Enter* Long John Silver, Dick, *and* Israel Hands.)

Silver. Come here, where it's quiet. You, Israel Hands, see if somebody's listening. (Hands *peers cautiously about.*) Now, Dick, you asked about my previous experience at sea. I sailed with Flint.

Dick. With Flint? Captain Flint? The pirate?

Silver. Not so loud, boy. I like to think of him as Captain Flint, gentleman of fortune. (Dick *nods.*) You're a smart lad, Dick, smart as paint. I saw that when I set eyes on you. (Dick *is flattered.*) Now, I'd like to talk to you, man to man.

Dick. Thank you, Long John.

Silver. Here's what it's like to be a gentleman of fortune. Oh, they're rough. They risk swinging! But when the cruise is done, they've got hundreds of pounds in their pockets. Not a few farthings like a sailor, like you, Dick. Think on it. Would you like to be a gentleman of fortune?

Dick. Don't know.

Silver. How would you like to go home with your pockets full of gold? (Dick *hesitates.*) How would you like a share of that buried treasure?

Dick. You mean the crew could get the buried treasure?

Silver. Under me they can, lad.

Dick. Are the rest of the crew with you?

Silver. That they are. I picked most of them. I have a way with me, I have. You can be sure of yourself on Long John Silver's ship.

Dick. Then I'm with you. Here's my hand. (Dick *extends hand.*)

SILVER. You're a brave lad, you are. And smart.

HANDS. I knew that Dick was a smart one. Now, let's grab the captain, the squire, the doctor, and that lad Jim Hawkins.

DICK (*laughs aloud*). Those landlubbers! Thought they'd get a treasure.

HANDS. What are we waitin' for?

SILVER (*firmly*). Israel Hand, your head's not much account. Never was. But you can hear. Leastways, your ears are big enough. You'll do as I say. Live like you always does, speak soft, keep sober, and wait—'til I give the word.

HANDS. I said when do we act?

SILVER. Like I said, when I can manage. We don't have the map, not yet. And we need the captain.

DICK. Why do we need him? We're all seamen here.

SILVER. We can steer a course, but we can't set one. We'll make the captain steer us back to the trade-lanes at least.

DICK. What of the others?

SILVER. We'll let them find the treasure. You understand that, Hands?

DICK. And then?

SILVER. Leave that to me, lad.

DICK. But in the end? What'll you do in the end?

SILVER. I'll explain that, Dick, when the time comes. Gentlemen of fortune have different ways. Some put them ashore, marooned. Others cut them up like so much pork. That's Flint's way.

HANDS. And my way! Dead men don't bite.

SILVER. Right you are! When I'm riding in my coach, I don't want sea-lawyers coming round disturbing me. And let's get one thing settled right now. I claim the squire for myself. I'll wring his calf's head off with my hands.

HANDS. I'd like to do that.

(Silver *notices that* Dick *seems to be getting sick*.)

SILVER. There, there, lad. It takes time to get to be a full-fledged gentleman of fortune. But you'll love the gold, lad. Think of that. Now, be a good lad. Reach into that barrel and get me an apple to wet my windpipe like.

(Dick *goes to the barrel as* Silver *starts to whisper to* Hands. *They glance at* Dick. *Before* Dick *has a chance to look into the barrel a cry comes from offstage.*)

LOOKOUT (*offstage*). Land, ho!

SILVER. To your posts, lads. (*Pirates exit.*)

JIM (*raising himself up from the barrel, the cat still in his arms*). Pirates! The captain's right. Every man in the crew is a PIRATE!

—*Pirates* is adapted from a chapter in TREASURE ISLAND by Robert Louis Stevenson.

PLAY A PART

JUSTICE FOR ALL

Introduction

Many Turkish tales tell of a wise judge, who either tricks a thief into admitting his guilt or identifies a culprit by some clever reasoning. Such a judge acts with dignity and is never hasty to reveal his thinking—until the problem is solved.

The crowd in this scene intensifies the drama. Every person listens intently to the words of the judge. All become disgusted with him when his actions seem foolish, and admire him when he solves his case.

The narrator is a crier who, with the aid of the goldsmith, explains what has happened before the scene opens.

Characters

CRIER	TOWNSPEOPLE
GOLDSMITH	SOLDIERS
ADULLA, the judge	

SCENE. *Street of an old Turkish city. Upstage center is a low door. A small platform is placed downstage. The curtain is drawn while the* Crier *is speaking. Turkish music, played before and after the* Crier *speaks, will give atmosphere.* Crier *steps before the curtain, reading a proclamation.*

CRIER. Come ye! Come ye! All who love justice, come ye! Come ye! Come ye! All who like strange sights, come ye! Come ye, all! Come ye, all! 'Tis the command of Adulla, the judge. Come ye, all. (*Lowers proclamation. Speaks in normal tone to audience.*) While the people are assembling, let me tell you what has happened. The goldsmith in this Turkish city has been robbed. Where are you, Goldsmith? (Goldsmith *enters and bows.*) Goldsmith, tell us what was taken.

GOLDSMITH. Jewels, gold, silver, money—everything.

CRIER. When were you robbed?

GOLDSMITH. Last night.

CRIER. How do you know the theft took place last night?

GOLDSMITH. At the end of the day I locked the front door of my shop. When I returned this morning, the back door of my shop was open.

CRIER. The back door? Was it strange to find the back door open?

GOLDSMITH. The back door of my shop has been closed for many months.

CRIER. Did anyone see the thief?

GOLDSMITH. No one saw the thief.

CRIER. Have you told these things to Adulla, the judge?

GOLDSMITH. I have, indeed. Adulla, the judge, has promised justice for all. He says he will name the thief today.

CRIER. How, sir?

GOLDSMITH. I know not. No one saw the thief. Excuse me, now. I must go to the back of my shop where Adulla has ordered all to assemble. (*Exits.*)

CRIER. Now we have the facts. The Goldsmith says that he has been robbed. No one saw the thief. There is only one clue, if clue it may be called. The back door that has been closed for many months was opened. Adulla, the wise judge, has promised to name the thief. Let us see what happens.

(*Curtain opens on a street scene. Some people are gathered around a fakir who is standing over a coiled rope. Veiled women walk across stage, some carrying bundles or water jars on their heads. Men and boys, each wearing a fez, walk by. Into their midst steps the* Crier. *Everyone stops to listen.*)

CRIER. Hear, ye! Hear, ye! Adulla, the wise judge, enters.

(*People lower heads as* Adulla *enters. He alone is wearing a turban. He mounts small platform. Others gather about, leaving the center of the stage vacant, especially the part in front of the door, which represents the back door to* Goldsmith's *shop. If music has been playing, it is stopped. All attention is focused on* Adulla, *who speaks first to the* Crier.)

ADULLA. Has everyone assembled?

CRIER. Everyone, as you commanded.

ADULLA. Good, for everyone seeks justice. We are here to consider the theft of jewels, money, and gold, all stolen from the goldsmith. Goldsmith, step forward. (Goldsmith *steps forward.*)

ADULLA. Goldsmith, what is your claim?

GOLDSMITH. I have been robbed.

ADULLA. Did you see the thief?

GOLDSMITH. No, sir, I did not.

ADULLA (*to crowd*). Did anyone see the thief?

CROWD. No. No. No. No. No.

ADULLA. When did the theft take place.

GOLDSMITH. During the night.

ADULLA. How do you know?

GOLDSMITH. When I locked my shop last night, the jewels, gold, and money were in their bags. When I opened the shop this morning, everything was gone. The back door was open. That door has not been used for months and months.

ADULLA. Is that your back door, the door that has not been used for months and months? (*Points to door.*)

GOLDSMITH. It is, sir.

ADULLA. Good people, you have heard the complaint of the goldsmith who was robbed of his jewels, gold, and money. I have promised justice to all. I shall keep my promise. Every evil-doer shall be punished.

CROWD. Good! Good! Down with evil! (Adulla *raises hands for quiet.*)

ADULLA. Behold this door. It is the duty of the door to keep out thieves. Last night the door failed to do its duty. The door shall be punished. Soldiers, five lashes on the door.

CROWD (*mumbling*). The door? Is he a wise judge, this Adulla? (*The crowd indicates by its actions that the judge must be crazy. The crowd is quiet again as* Adulla *raises his hands to speak.*)

ADULLA. Step back! (*People step back from the door.*) Soldiers, do your duty. (*Some soldiers hold back the crowd. One soldier steps forward and lashes door.* Adulla *steps off the platform. Goes to door.*) Now, door, are you willing to tell me who entered here last night? (*Waits.*) Name the thief! If you are afraid to speak aloud, whisper to me. (*He puts his ear to the door, then returns to the stand.*) The door speaks nonsense! Soldier, give the door five more lashes.

(*Crowd murmurs discontent as soldier again lashes door.* Adulla *returns to the door.*)

ADULLA. Door, will you now tell me who entered here last night. (*Listens.*) Name the thief. (*Listens to door. Returns to stand.*) The door still talks nonsense. The door tells me the thief is in the crowd. (*Everyone looks at his neighbors.*) The door tells me that the thief has dust and cobwebs on his fez. (*One man lifts his hand to dust the top of his fez.* Adulla *points to the man with the raised hand.*) Grab him! Thief! Grab him! (*Soldiers grab man and bring him to* Adulla. Thief *falls on knees before* Adulla.)

THIEF. Mercy! Mercy! I'll return the jewels, the gold, the money. (*Takes out bag.*) Everything is here. (*Hands bag to* Adulla.) Mercy, mercy!

ADULLA. I promised justice, not mercy. Soldiers, take this thief away. Give him as many lashes as you gave the door. (*Soldiers exit with screaming thief. Soon all is quiet as crowd looks at* Adulla *in wonderment.*)

ADULLA. Goldsmith, are these your jewels, gold, and money? (*Hands bag to* Goldsmith *who examines contents quickly.*)

GOLDSMITH. Indeed, they are, sir. Thank you, sir.

ADULLA. I promised justice. I administered justice.

GOLDSMITH. You did indeed, sir. Now may I ask how you knew the thief?

ADULLA. Think, Goldsmith. What happens when a door is left closed for many months.

GOLDSMITH. Dust and cobwebs collect, sir.

ADULLA. Who knew that the door was covered with cobwebs?

GOLDSMITH. The man who opened it, sir.

ADULLA. Why would he open the door?

GOLDSMITH. Why—why, to steal the jewels, gold, and money.

ADULLA. Therefore, who wanted to remove cobwebs and dirt from his fez?

GOLDSMITH. The thief!

ADULLA. Exactly. When I saw one man raise his hand to his fez to brush away dust and cobwebs, I knew that man to be the thief.

GOLDSMITH. Justice was done. Allah be praised. (*Raises hands and bows.*)

ADULLA AND CROWD. Allah be praised! (*Curtain is lowered as they are bowing.*)

—*Justice for All* is based on "The Wise Judge" from FOLKLORE FROM FOREIGN LANDS by Catherine T. Bryce. New York: Nelson and Company, 1913.

THE GOLDEN TOOTH

Introduction

Dame Van Pelt in this playlet is a woman of many moods. Prim and proper at one moment, she flares out in anger the next. She bursts out crying, and then turns off her tears. Why is she angry, rather than sad, when Captain Kidd tells her that her husband was a pirate, and is dead?

She is pretending all the time. She is trying to cover up the fact that she has only one love: the love of gold. She stops pretending and becomes her scared self only when she realizes that her selfishness—her love of gold—may ruin her.

Captain Kidd was a real person; but legends about him are more numerous than historical accounts. Whether or not he had a gold tooth makes little difference. In this playlet, based on a legend, he makes Dame Van Pelt think that he has a golden tooth that turns everything he bites to gold.

In *The Golden Tooth,* Captain Kidd is a haughty, ill-mannered man who understands Dame Van Pelt completely. He enjoys his ability to break through her playacting and make her miserable.

The officers and soldiers act like gentlemen and are bewildered by Dame Van Pelt's playacting. The sooner they can do their duty and get out, the better.

Try to create a haunting atmosphere. It will help the audience feel that maybe Captain Kidd did come in from the sea on a stormy night and put a curse on a Dame Van Pelt. Emphasize the pantomime as well as the lines that help the audience understand the significance of the golden tooth as a symbol of the greed for gold.

Characters

DAME VAN PELT — OFFICER OF THE LAW
SAILOR — SOLDIERS

SCENE. *Comfortable back parlor of* Dame Van Pelt, *in a waterfront town about 1700. Center stage is a small round table, with a straight-backed chair on the right and a "company" chair on the left. A door center back leads into a smokehouse in which are placed in advance two objects wrapped in gold foil to look like large hunks of gold. An exit left leads to the street. There should also be a window with drapes, or drapes alone just to represent a window.*

Sound effects include a triangle, or some other instrument that can be struck for a town clock, and a wind-maker, if possible. An amplifier to help carry offstage voices will help.

As the scene opens, Dame Van Pelt *is sitting primly in the straight-backed chair, looking at a plate of cookies and bread on the table. Wind howls outside.*

DAME VAN PELT. Now let me see. Shall I have a cookie? Or shall I have a piece of bread before I go to bed. Which shall it be? Cookie? Or bread? Oh, that wind! I hate nights alone when the wind howls. (*She rises, goes to window, looks out, pulls drapes together tightly.*) That's better. (*Pulls shawl around her shoulders.*) What a night! The wind blows right through me, like a ghost coming out of the sea. Well, for more pleasant thoughts. (*Sits down.*) Which shall it be? A cookie? Or bread?

SAILOR (*offstage*). Ho, there!

DAME VAN PELT (*startled*). Who's there? (*She rises.*)

SAILOR (*offstage*). Does Dame Van Pelt live here?

DAME VAN PELT. I am Dame Van Pelt.

SAILOR. Wife of Jan Van Pelt?

DAME VAN PELT. Yes.

SAILOR. Then let me in! (*No answer.*) Let me in out of the rain, I say!

DAME VAN PELT. I don't know your voice. (*Clock offstage strikes eight.*) Did you hear that? The town clock strikes eight o'clock. Be gone!

SAILOR. I bring news of your husband.

DAME VAN PELT. My husband! (*She rushes to the door. A rough-looking sailor enters wearing a long cloak. He rudely steps to center stage, stamping his wet feet.* Dame Van Pelt *is horrified and speechless. He takes off his cloak. Shakes it as if shaking off water.*)

DAME VAN PELT. It's wet! You're wet! My floor is wet!

SAILOR (*mocking her*). Of course it's wet. Very wet! It's raining. Everything is wet. (*He hands her his cloak as if she were a servant. She doesn't want to take it, but she doesn't know what else to do*).

DAME VAN PELT. It's wet, and it's heavy. (*At last she hangs it on a peg, very much upset. In the meantime, he sits down in the company chair and crosses his legs rudely.* Dame Van Pelt *is furious. At last she pulls herself together and sits primly in the straight-backed chair at the table.*)

DAME VAN PELT. My husband? You said you had news of my husband.

SAILOR. So you are the wid— I mean wife of my good friend Jan Van Pelt. A mad fellow!

DAME VAN PELT. Mad fellow? You say mad? My husband is steadfast, noble, generous, honorable—

SAILOR (*interrupting*). Maybe at home, but at sea—

DAME VAN PELT. Sir, how dare you speak this way of my husband? You must be thinking of some other Van Pelt. There is Dirk Van Pelt and Johan Van Pelt and—

SAILOR. No, no. I am thinking of the right Van Pelt. Jan Van Pelt, your husband. He gave me this, and your address just before he left. (*He hands her a small bag with a paper attached.*)

DAME VAN PELT (*looking at paper on bag*). The address is in Jan's handwriting. (*Opens bag.*) Gold! Enough gold to last until spring. (*Places bag in her lap, but hangs on to it.*) But what is the news of Jan?

SAILOR. Well, when he was about to board a ship to capture—

DAME VAN PELT. Capture? Capture what? There's no war.

SAILOR. Well, then, to loot.

DAME VAN PELT. Loot! Jan, loot?

SAILOR (*rising*). Ha! Ha! Ha! (*Takes a few paces. Turns and faces her directly.*) So you didn't know Jan was a pirate?

DAME VAN PELT. Jan, a pirate? (*Rises.*) Wait until he gets home!

SAILOR. Now, Madam, don't tell me that you didn't know Jan was a pirate. (*She remains motionless.*) You wanted a fine home, pretty clothes.

DAME VAN PELT. Of course.

SAILOR. And you thought that your husband bought all this with the pay of a poor sailor?

DAME VAN PELT. I never asked.

SAILOR. Why ask now? Jan is at the bottom of the sea.

DAME VAN PELT. What did you say?

SAILOR. Jan was killed on our last venture. (*He sits calmly. She leans over the table and yells at him.*)

DAME VAN PELT. "*Our* last venture!" Jan Van Pelt and *you!* (Sailor *nods.*) Sir, how dare you come into my house dripping wet, seat yourself in my best chair, and tell me casually that my husband was a pirate! And now you say he is dead! Who are you?

(Sailor *rises slowly. Throws back shoulders.*)

SAILOR. I am Captain Kidd.

DAME VAN PELT. Captain Kidd! No! No! (*She falls on her knees before him and pleads for mercy.*) Spare me! Spare me!

SAILOR. Rise, madam. (*She does so.*) I have no desire to kill you. You have no gold. (*She turns her back to him.*) All the world knows that Captain Kidd kills only for gold. (*She shrugs her shoulders.*) Don't think harshly of me. All men love gold. All women love gold, too.

DAME VAN PELT. I hate gold! (*She sits in straight-backed chair.*)

SAILOR. Oh, do you really? (*He sits in company chair and*

leans over the table as he talks.) Supposing I were to tell you about a way to get gold without killing, without looting, and without working. Supposing I were to tell you about a magic way to get gold.

DAME VAN PELT (*scornfully*). Magic?

SAILOR. Supposing I were to tell you about my golden tooth.

DAME VAN PELT (*excitedly*). Golden tooth? (*She corrects herself.*) Captain Kidd, I'll not listen to you. I know there is a curse on everything you touch. (*She hesitates.*) But tell me about your golden tooth. Just to pass the time, tell me about your tooth.

SAILOR (*slowly*). Whatever I bite with my golden tooth turns to gold.

DAME VAN PELT. Food, sticks, anything you bite turns to gold? I don't believe it.

SAILOR (*mysteriously*). You believe in spells. You love gold. Why not believe in a golden tooth?

OFFICER (*offstage*). Dame Van Pelt! Dame Van Pelt! Are you in?

DAME VAN PELT. Yes, I am in. (*To* Sailor) Quickly! Get into the smokehouse. Hide behind the hams and cheeses. (*Points to door upstage.* Sailor *grabs his cloak, dashes into closet.*)

OFFICER. Let us in! It's the law.

DAME VAN PELT. In a minute. In a minute. It's eight o'clock. I was about to retire. Just a minute. (*As soon as she is sure that the* Sailor *is in the smokehouse, she opens outside door and with great dignity, greets the* Officer *and* Soldiers *warmly.*)

DAME VAN PELT. Come in! Come in out of the rain!

(Officer *and* Soldiers *enter.* Dame Van Pelt *stands near her straight-backed chair.* Officer *comes downstage.*)

OFFICER. I'm sorry to disturb you, ma'am. We are looking for Captain Kidd.

DAME VAN PELT (*trembling*). Captain Kidd? No! No!

OFFICER. Don't be frightened, ma'am. We know he's in port. We must search every house. (Dame Van Pelt *acts as if she may faint.*) Just look around, men. Don't disturb a thing. Poor soul, all alone. Her husband is at sea.

ONE SOLDIER (*at smokehouse door*). How about in here? (Dame Van Pelt *rushes to the smokehouse door.*)

DAME VAN PELT. No, no! Please not in here! It's the smoke room. I just placed my ham and cheese in the smoke room. (*She sobs.*) If you open the door now, the hams and cheese will spoil. I'll starve if you destroy my hams and cheese. Please, don't open this door.

OFFICER. Calm yourself. No one will open that door.

SOLDIER. We cured our hams some time ago.

OFFICER. I know, so did we. But the dame's husband is at sea. Time schedules differ. Just look around, men. (*They start to search.*) Quickly!

DAME VAN PELT. Thank you, sir. Thank you. And God bless you. You are brave. You are considerate. You wouldn't let a woman starve. (Officer, *embarrassed goes downstage as she follows him.*) Oh, sir, if you only could know what it's like to be the wife of a sailor away at sea. (*She tries to cry on his shoulder. He pulls away. Doesn't know what to do with all the attention.*)

OFFICER. Calm yourself. Calm yourself. I hate to see a woman cry. (*To* Soldiers.) Let's go, men. The woman is upset. (*To* Dame Van Pelt.) Thank you, ma'am. And good night.

DAME VAN PELT. Good night, and thank you again. You don't know what you have done to help me.

(Officer *and* Soldiers *exit. She looks out of the window to make sure that they are gone. Runs to the smoke-room door.*)

DAME VAN PELT. It's safe. Come out.

(Captain Kidd *comes out. He is wearing his cloak and carrying two big pieces of gold, one as big as a ham, the other as big as a cheese. He strides downstage, left. She follows and stands downstage right, staring in amazement at the gold.*)

DAME VAN PELT. My ham! My cheese! They're gold!

SAILOR. Remember the golden tooth?

DAME VAN PELT. You bit my ham—my cheese? With your golden tooth? They turned to gold?

SAILOR. I told you. Whatever I bite with my golden tooth turns to gold. (*Places gold objects on table. Announces dramatically.*) They are yours, for saving me!

DAME VAN PELT. Mine? All that gold is mine? (*He nods. She lifts objects and holds them as if weighing them. Puts them down angrily.*) Now what can I do with big hunks of gold? People would say that I stole them. (*He smiles.*) Or worse yet. That I made a deal with pirates who had melted it down. Take your gold.

SAILOR. Very well. I'll keep my gold and leave by golden tooth with you.

DAME VAN PELT. I don't want your golden tooth.

SAILOR. Everything you bite will turn to gold. (*He tosses golden tooth on table. She looks at it. Touches it. Puts it down again. He watches her, amused. Picks up his chunks of gold.*) Goodbye, madam. (*Goes toward door.*)

DAME VAN PELT. Wait! Your golden tooth. You left your golden tooth.

SAILOR. Keep it. Everything you bite with it will turn to gold. (*Exits.*)

(Dame Van Pelt *sits down slowly. Looks at tooth.*) Everything I bite with it will turn to gold. (*Picks up cookie.*) Now if I took a little bite, I could sell a little bit of gold. (*Breaks off a little piece of cookie.*) No one would ask how I got that much gold. (*Puts down cookie bit. Picks up tooth.*) I wonder if it fits. It can't hurt to try. (*Appears to slip it over her own tooth.*) A perfect fit. (*Picks up a bit of cookie again.*) Everything I bite with it will turn to gold. (*Gets angry with herself.*) Nonsense, I should not use a golden tooth. (*Tugs on tooth.*) It won't come off! The golden tooth! It won't come off! (*Stands up and starts to pace floor.*) It won't come off! Everything I bite will turn to gold. I'll starve to death! Gold cookie. Gold ham! Gold cheese. I'll starve to death! (*Becomes hysterical. Faces audience downstage center.*) The curse of Captain Kidd. I'll starve to death because of gold! (*Screams.*) Ohhhhh! (*She sinks into chair, throws her head on the table, and sobs.*) Ohhhhh!

SAILOR (*offstage*). The greed for gold. The curse of Captain Kidd. The greed for gold.

(*The words are repeated over and over like the sound of the wind.* Dame Van Pelt *continues to sob hysterically without tasting a bite of food to test the spell of the tooth. Curtain is pulled on the haunting scene.*)

PLAYLETS AND DRAMATIC SCENES

REBECCA OF SUNNYBROOK FARM

Introduction

Read the opening chapters of *Rebecca of Sunnybrook Farm* by Kate Douglas Wiggin in order to understand the three characters in this dramatic scene. They are Miranda, whose "heart is used only for pumping and circulating blood" (Miranda speaks crisply and curtly); Jane, who is so soft that there is danger she will "leak out of the house and into the dooryard" (Jane speaks in a softer, more pleasant voice); and Rebecca, their young imaginative niece with eyes "like faith—'the substance of things hoped for, the evidence of things not seen.'" Or, as the coach driver reasoned, "a bird of a very different feather from those whom he was accustomed to in his daily life." Until the very end of the scene Rebecca is excited and anxious to share the description of her home with her aunts. At the very end Rebecca is solemn and sad, but firm when she repeats for the second time, "I'm coming."

Because this is a dramatic scene from a book, not a full-length play, the characters do not change in their attitudes toward each other or toward life. This scene offers an opportunity to portray contrasts in personality.

Characters

MIRANDA SAWYER, unmarried woman between fifty and sixty years old

JANE SAWYER, her unmarried sister

REBECCA ROWENA RANDALL, their niece

SCENE. *The Sawyer home, a big brick house in Riverboro, Maine, about 1900.* Miranda *and* Jane *are in the parlor or kitchen, awaiting the arrival of their young niece* Rebecca. Jane *is seated downstage right, embroidering.* Miranda *is dusting an already spotlessly clean room. When excited, she polishes with extra vigor a shiny candlestick or dish on a small table downstage left. A water pitcher with water in it and an empty vase stand on a table, chest, or desk upstage left. An outside door opens upstage center. Exit to other parts of the house is right. A braided rug is placed near each exit.*

MIRANDA. Well, she should be here any minute. Rebecca Rowena Randall. Where did her folks get a name like that?

JANE. From *Ivanhoe,* as you have been told many times.

MIRANDA. Rebecca Rowena. At least Rebecca is a civilized name. I shall think of the Bible, not *Ivanhoe,* when I speak to Rebecca. (*Starts to dust again. Stops almost at once.*) Why did Aurelia send Rebecca? Why didn't she send Hannah, the one we asked for?

JANE (*putting down sewing*). Miranda Sawyer, you know very well that when we wrote to our dear widowed sister Aurelia we offered to take any one of the older girls—Hannah, Rebecca, or even little Jenny. We offered to give her an education so that she could go to work and help pay off the mortgage on their farm.

MIRANDA. Mortgage! Oh, don't say that word, Jane Sawyer. Someone might hear that Aurelia *Sawyer* has a mortgage. Aurelia may be Mrs. Randall, but she is still Aurelia Sawyer.

JANE. Miranda, we offered to help our sister, who is trying to bring up seven young ones without the help of a husband.

MIRANDA. I still say she should have sent the oldest one, Hannah. Hannah is sensible and capable. She didn't say a word when we were there. On the other hand, Rebecca—(*Sighs just to think of it.*) Rebecca was as noisy as a magpie, and just about as useful!

JANE. She was a mite of a thing when we saw her three years ago, and she's had time to improve.

MIRANDA. And time to grow worse.

JANE. Won't it be a privilege to put her on the right track?

MIRANDA. I don't know about the privilege part. It'll be a chore. If her mother hasn't got her on the right track now, she won't take to it all of a sudden. If she causes as much work as she used to, we'll never get any rest.

JANE. She'll make a difference, but she may be more biddable than we think.

MIRANDA. She'll mind when she's spoken to, biddable or not!

JANE. I know you have a heart, Miranda; but sometimes I think it is used only for pumping and circulating blood.

MIRANDA. You're soft, Jane, always were and always will be. If it weren't for me keeping you stiffened up, you'd leak out of the house and into the dooryard.

(*A knock is heard on the door.*)

JANE. Land of Liberty! There she is. (Jane *puts down her sewing, straightens her dress, smooths her hair. Smiles as* Miranda *goes to door and opens it.* Rebecca *enters demurely, holding wilted flowers in her hand.*)

REBECCA. Aunt Miranda, Aunt Jane, I am your niece, Rebecca Rowena Randall.

(Jane *and* Miranda *speak at the same time, but* Miranda's *voice drowns out* Jane's.)

JANE (*extending arms in greeting*). Rebecca!

MIRANDA. I guessed as much. Come near the light so we can see you. (*They come downstage.* Rebecca, *much frightened, stands between her aunts.* Jane *kisses her sweetly.* Miranda *stands looking at her.*)

REBECCA. I brought some flowers.

MIRANDA. You needn't have bothered. The garden's always full of flowers when the time comes.

REBECCA. These flowers are from Sunnybrook Farm.

JANE. Sunnybrook Farm?

MIRANDA. You mean the Randall farm. I guess it makes no difference what you call a place, as long as you know where it is.

REBECCA. But it does make a difference. When I say "Sunnybrook Farm," what does it make you think of?

JANE. I suppose there's a brook nearby.

REBECCA. You're warm, but not hot. There's a brook, but not a common brook. It has young trees and baby bushes on each side of it, and it's a shallow chattering little brook with a white sandy bottom and lots of little shiny pebbles. Whenever there's a bit of sunshine, the brook catches it, and it's full of sparkles the livelong day.

JANE. How beautiful. (*She sighs as she accepts flowers and goes to back of room, fills vase with water, and puts flowers into it.* Miranda *stiffens.*)

MIRANDA. The livelong day! Who would watch a brook the livelong day? Come, Rebecca, I'll take you to your room. Remember to use the back stairs. (*She turns to go, assuming that* Rebecca *is following her.*) We never use the front stairs because of the carpet. Might wear out the carpet if we used it too often. Oh yes, always rub your feet on this braided rug. (*Exits, still talking.*) Don't ever track in mud. Never lie on the bed in the daytime. You'll muss up the feathers and dirty the pillows. (*Her voice trails off, but can be heard giving directions about use of towels, etc. As* Miranda *is leaving,* Jane *brings the vase and flowers downstage to the little table left. She and* Rebecca *stand admiring them and arranging them. Suddenly an offstage voice rends the air.*)

MIRANDA. REBECCA!

(Rebecca *jumps like a frightened animal.*)

REBECCA. Yes, Aunt Miranda. (*Throws back her shoulders bravely.*) I'm coming. (*Exits, stiff and proper.*) I'm coming.

—Adapted from REBECCA OF SUNNYBROOK FARM by Kate Douglas Wiggin, New York: Grosset and Dunlap, 1903.

REAL-LIFE DRAMA

The real-life drama given in this section includes skits, playlets, and dramatic scenes. The actors must decide which characters are comic "types," familiar to all of us, and which characters are individuals. Of course, a "type" character can and should have individuality, and a historic individual can be comic in a certain situation.

Before you start to work on a real-life dramatic skit, scene, or playlet, study the historic period in which it takes place. Study the customs and the general attitudes of people. How did workmen feel toward each other? Did common people tend to regard leaders with admiration? How did people feel about popular superstitions or about current events? You may not find all the answers but you can develop understanding that will help you re-create historic roles.

Read all you can about the historic characters that are mentioned. What big ideas interested them? How old were they when the event in the scene took place? Were they already famous at that time? Was a certain man occasionally inclined to tell a joke, or was he always serious and ponderous in his speech?

Don't try to assume the dialect of a certain geographic region or a bygone speech pattern. Give an impression by the manner in which you say today's words. For example, trying to use "thee" and "thou" in a Quaker play could hamper an actor whose main purpose should be to stress Quaker concepts of brotherly love which include common sense.

When you know enough about a period and its people to feel at ease in a role, try to put yourself into the shoes of a historic person, real or imaginary, and act out a historic situation.

IMPOSSIBLE! UNACCEPTABLE! PREPOSTEROUS!

Introduction

Modern highways are just that—modern, something new. Seventy-five years ago even the best of highways were likely to be full of long muddy stretches during the spring thaws. What to do when a coach got stuck in the mud was the driver's problem, but sometimes became the problem of the passengers, too.

In this skit, actors pantomime riding in a horse-drawn coach that gets stuck in the mud. Imagine their disgust at being caught in an "impossible" situation with an "impossible" driver who insists on waiting until the mud dries out unless—and that's the point of the skit.

Before working on the entire skit, pantomime walking in mud. Remember, the passengers are all dressed up. Men are wearing long tight pants, and women long skirts. How do you think they feel about getting mud on their clothing? How do they show their feelings?

REAL-LIFE DRAMA

Characters

Narrator	Mr. Gibbs	Passengers
Mr. DeCamp, driver of DeCamp coach	Mr. Almsted	
	Miss Elliott	
	Mrs. Brydon	
	Other Passengers (*if desired*)	

Scene. *A coach on a muddy road in the spring of 1888. Chairs represent the coach, shown sideview. A tall stool is placed in front to represent the driver's seat. Two rows of chairs, facing each other, with a space for entering in the middle, provide seats for passengers.*

Narrator. Our scene is Essex County, New Jersey, in the spring of 1888, after the famed blizzard of that year.

We ask you to imagine that these chairs and stool represent the DeCamp Stagecoach that ran from Orange to Livingston. The passengers will, of course, occupy the inside of the coach while the driver, Mr. DeCamp, will ride on top to drive the horses. Here comes Mr. DeCamp, followed by the passengers. (DeCamp *enters, followed by men passengers.*)

Mr. DeCamp. All aboard! All aboard for Livingston. (*Passengers line up.*)

Mr. Gibbs. Good morning. (*Hands ticket to* DeCamp.)

Mr. DeCamp. Good morning, sir.

Mr. Gibbs. Nice day.

Mr. DeCamp. Fortunately.

Mr. Gibbs. Fortunately, indeed, after last winter. (*Enters coach.*)

Mr. Almsted. Good morning. How are the roads? (*Hands ticket to* DeCamp.)

DeCamp. Hard to tell, sir. We'll find out. (Almsted *boards coach.*)

Miss Elliott. Mr. DeCamp, confidentially, how are the roads?

Mr. DeCamp. Confidentially, I don't know. We had a bad winter. Lots of snow. Big thaw.

Miss Elliott. And that means muddy roads.

Mr. DeCamp. I know.

Miss Elliott (*to companion*). Mrs. Brydon, what shall we do?

Mrs. Brydon. What can we do? We have to go to Livingston. There is only one way to get there. We have to take the coach.

Miss Elliott. Mr. DeCamp, are you sure you can get us to Livingston?

MR. DECAMP. I'll get you there sooner or later.

MRS. BRYDON. Well, I hope it's sooner. My niece is getting married, and I want to attend the wedding. Come, Natalie, let's board. (*Gives tickets to* DeCamp. *Sits in chair with* Miss Elliott *nearer audience. If there are other passengers, they also board quickly, giving tickets to* DeCamp *and making remarks about the big thaw.* Mr. DeCamp *mounts stool in front of chairs. Picks up reins. Calls* "Giddap" *to horses. Starts to whistle or sing* "Oh, Susanna." *He and passengers jog up and down. Some get weary. Some are excited about scenery. Soon* DeCamp *realizes that horses are having trouble. Pulls reins tight.*)

DECAMP. Steady, boys. Gee! Haw! Pull. (*Everyone jerks, then sits still. Passengers look at each other bewildered.*)

MR. ALMSTED (*looking out of window*). I say, sir. What is the trouble?

MR. DECAMP. We seem to be stuck in the mud. (*Gets down from stool. Pantomimes wading through mud. Goes back to coach.*)

MISS ELLIOTT. Stuck in the mud? Impossible! What's to be done? Impossible!

MR. DECAMP. Just one thing. Everybody get out. Push the coach out of the mud.

MISS ELLIOTT. Impossible!

MR. GIBBS. Us! Push the coach?

MR. DECAMP. Yes, sir. We are mired down deep. There's only one way to get out of this mud. Everybody has to help push the coach.

MR. GIBBS. Sir, may I remind you that we paid for our transportation from Orange to Livingston.

OTHER PASSENGERS. Yes!

MR. ALMSTED. It is your duty to get us to Livingston.

MR. DECAMP. If you want to get to Livingston, you'll have to help push this coach out of the mud.

MISS ELLIOTT. Impossible!

MR. GIBBS. Unacceptable!

MR. ALMSTED. Preposterous!

MRS. BRYDON (*standing at her seat*). I can't push a coach. I'm all dressed for a wedding.

MISS ELLIOTT. Mr. DeCamp, you distinctly said that you would get us to Livingston.

MR. DECAMP. I said I would get you to Livingston sooner or later.

(*As passengers discuss situation angrily,* DeCamp *calmly climbs into the driver's seat, takes out a small book, and begins to read to himself, smiling and nodding.*)

DECAMP. Beautiful! Lovely! (*Passengers are increasingly restless. They gesture as they express their disgust and despair to each other.*)

MR. ALMSTED. Sir, what are you doing?

MR. DECAMP. I'm reading. Listen to this,

My hair is gray, but not with years;
Nor grew it white
In a single night,
As men's have grown from sudden fears.

MR. GIBBS. What on earth?

MR. DECAMP. Oh, it's "The Prisoner of Chillon"—Byron, you know.

MR. GIBBS. Yes, I know. I know what you're reading. But why are you reading?

DECAMP. I like to read while I wait.

MR. GIBBS. What are you waiting for?

MR. DECAMP. I'm waiting for the mud to dry out.

ALL. Mud to dry out?

MR. DECAMP. Yes, I'm waiting for the mud to dry out. Ladies and gentlement, the DeCamp coach is stuck in the mud.

ALL. We know!

MR. DECAMP. The horses cannot pull the coach out of the mud. The passengers will not help push the coach out of the mud.

I cannot push the coach alone. So—I'm waiting for the mud to dry out. (*Continues to read as passengers protest.*)

"My limbs are bowed, though not with toil—"

MISS ELLIOTT. Impossible!

MR. GIBBS. Unacceptable!

MR. ALMSTED. Preposterous!

MRS. BRYDON. Ridiculous!

(Mr. DeCamp *pays no attention to the exclaiming passengers. At last* Mr. Gibbs *rolls up his pants legs, gets out of the coach slowly, pantomimes wading through the mud to the back of the coach and pretends to push.* Mr. DeCamp *puts book away, picks up reins and encourages horses to pull. Other passengers follow as curtain closes.*

If there is no curtain, passengers line up in back to push coach. Mr. DeCamp *encourages horses to pull. Everyone realizes when coach is out of mud, passengers get back into coach.* Mr. DeCamp *drives as in the beginning and at last calls,* "Livingston." *All get out, brushing off mud, etc.*

Actors may end this skit in another way if they so wish. As passengers are complaining loudly, Mr. Gibbs *calls,* "Quiet!" *Then says,* "Let's ask the audience what to do." *All agree.* "Audience," *says* Mr. Gibbs, "shall we push the coach or wait for the mud to dry out?" *After a moment, he calls* "Quiet!" *Then he either announces,* "The audience says we must wait." *Passengers slump into their seats. Or he announces,* "The audience says to push." *In that event, the passengers follow the original directions for the skit.*)

—*Impossible! Unacceptable! Preposterous!* is adapted with permission from an account of the event which appeared in "Tel-News," May 1968, published by the New Jersey Bell Telephone Company.

PLAY A PART

WHERE THERE ARE NO SNAGS

Introduction

At this period in his life Abe Lincoln was a shy young man with a backwoods appearance. It took courage to step before the well-dressed people and apply for a job. However, he showed his humble politeness and also his ability to think quickly and match his wits against those of the frustrated captain.

The captain is businesslike, worried, and more than a little annoyed by people who keep talking to him. It is hard for him not to lose his temper.

Every member of the crowd must help create the atmosphere of annoyance and, later, relief when the captain hires the young man.

Characters

CAPTAIN	FUSSY LADY
YOUNG MAN	OTHER PEOPLE

SCENE. *A dock on the Mississippi River at New Orleans before the Civil War.* Captain *stands center stage, very much worried. People are milling back and forth, asking,* "When does this steamboat sail?" "How can we get there on time?" *and so on.*

FUSSY LADY (*to* Captain). Tell me, Captain, exactly when will we sail?

CAPTAIN. I've explained to everyone. We'll sail when the pilot arrives.

FUSSY LADY. When will that be, sir?

CAPTAIN. Lady, if I knew I'd tell all of you.

YOUNG MAN (*stepping out of crowd*). Excuse me, lady. Morning, sir. Are you looking for a pilot?

CAPTAIN. Am I looking for a pilot? Indeed I am! I am looking for that good-for-nothing Bates. Should have been here an hour ago. Passengers waiting. Crew ready. A load of pigs going north.

I ask you, what will I do with a load of pigs if I run out of feed? I can't get started. Where is Bates?

YOUNG MAN. Excuse me again, sir. Have you considered hiring another pilot?

CAPTAIN. Another pilot. Where would I get another pilot?

YOUNG MAN. Here, sir.

CAPTAIN. Suppose you are a pilot. Do you know anything about this river?

YOUNG MAN. Yes, sir, I know a lot about this river.

CAPTAIN. Do you know anything about its currents?

YOUNG MAN. Yes, sir, I know a lot about its currents.

CAPTAIN. Do you know where all the snags are?

YOUNG MAN. No, sir, can't say I know where all the snags are.

CAPTAIN. You don't know where the snags are? How can you pilot a steamboat on the Mississippi River when you don't know where the snags are?

YOUNG MAN (*speaking slowly*). Well, sir, I know where the snags aren't. I'll sail where there are no snags.

CAPTAIN (*liking answer*). Sail where there are no snags. That's a good idea. (*Crowd agrees.*) Perhaps you are a good pilot. What's your name?

YOUNG MAN. Abe Lincoln, sir. Abe Lincoln of Illinois.

CAPTAIN (*shaking his hand*). Abe Lincoln, you're hired! All aboard! (*Crowd cheers.*)

WHAT IS IT?

Introduction

This skit is based on a reportedly true story about how Mr. Charles Darwin, the famous naturalist, turned the tables and played a joke on a group of boys who had tried to fool him. In order to portray Mr. Darwin, read about him. Then try to act as dignified as this professional man, who was willing to uphold his opinions, often controversial, any time at any place.

In our skit Mr. Darwin approaches the boys' "problem" in a mock professional manner, never revealing for one moment that he knows that the boys are trying to trick him. His exit is as dignified as his entrance.

The boys are about to burst with excitement because they know about the trick. They restrain themselves, however, until the joke is played on Archie, who had originated the mischief. Even then they must be quiet enough to allow the audience to hear Percy's last line, "You can't fool Mr. Darwin."

Both Archie and Mr. Darwin have excellent opportunities for pantomime. Time these little scenes in such a way that they add suspense to the skit, without becoming boring.

There may be either English boys or girls in the play. The skit can be produced with as few as two or three children, or as many as is practical. Do not try to use an English accent; but when you are adlibbing avoid American expressions such as "O.K." or "You fooled him, man!" and so on. If you use girls in the cast, they should not wear slacks or shorts which would have shocked people in nineteenth-century England. Avoid using obviously modern equipment, such as glue in a plastic bottle.

Characters

ARCHIE, LESTER, PERCY — English boys
MR. CHARLES DARWIN
OTHER BOYS

SCENE. *A park in England, sometime between 1860 and 1875. A small picnic table or box stands center stage. On it are pincers, glue pot with small stick in it, heavy paper, pins, and so on.* Archie *is happily humming or whistling as he mounts an insect, or parts of insects, on paper. He picks up a bit with tweezers, holds it in place with pins, dabs a bit of glue on the paper, presses the object carefully with a finger. After each move he stands back and admires his work.* Lester *enters unnoticed and stands watching* Archie.

LESTER. I say, Archie, what are you doing?

ARCHIE. Can't you tell? (*He continues work.*)

LESTER. No.

ARCHIE. Good.

LESTER. Good? (*Watches a moment more.*) All right. I know you are mounting something. Mr. Darwin taught us how to mount insects. But I don't know what you are mounting.

ARCHIE. Splendid. (Lester *looks bewildered.*) You don't know what it is, and that's the point.

LESTER. What point?

ARCHIE. I am going to fool Mr. Darwin.

LESTER. You can't fool Mr. Charles Darwin. He knows more about nature than anyone else in the world.

ARCHIE. However, he does not know about this bug. See, I took the body of a centipede, the wings of a butterfly, the head of a beetle, and the legs of a grasshopper. (*Stands back and looks at his work.*)

LESTER. I say! That does look great.

ARCHIE. Now when Mr. Darwin comes along, I'll say, (*He pantomimes as he talks.*) "Good morning, Mr. Darwin. We caught this in the field. Can you tell us what it is?" Then I'll show him this bug. (Other Boys *enter.*)

LESTER. Chipper!

PERCY. What's chipper?

LESTER. Archie is going to fool Mr. Darwin.

PERCY. Fool Mr. Darwin? You can't fool Mr. Charles Darwin. He knows more about insects than anyone else in the world. I know. I've worked in fields with him.

ARCHIE. All right. Look here. (*He holds up paper.* Percy *looks at it.*) Well, what is it?

PERCY. I don't know. (Other Boys *crowd around to look at it.*)

ARCHIE. You don't know. That's good.

LESTER. Tell them, Archie. Let them in on the joke.

ARCHIE. I took the body of a centipede, the wings of a butterfly, the head of a beetle, and the legs of a grasshopper.

BOYS. Splendid. Looks real enough.

PERCY. I still say, "You can't fool Mr. Darwin."

LESTER. Shhh—here comes Mr. Darwin now. (*Boys are very solemn.* Mr. Darwin *enters.* Archie *takes his mounting and advances toward* Mr. Darwin. *They meet center downstage.*)

ALL BOYS. Good morning, Mr. Darwin.

MR. DARWIN. Good morning, boys. How are you this fine morning?

ARCHIE. Very well, sir. But we do have a problem.

MR. DARWIN. A problem? Can I help you?

ARCHIE. Perhaps, sir. We caught this in the field. Can you

tell us what it is? (*Hands mounted bug to* Mr. Darwin.)

(Mr. Darwin *accepts mounting. Examines it closely, shaking his head. Takes out granny glasses or magnifying glass. Looks again. Appears puzzled. Boys are about to burst with excitement, but grow serious when* Mr. Darwin *looks up.*)

MR. DARWIN. Did this hum when it was flying?

ARCHIE. Yes, sir, it hummed when it was flying (*Boys nod*).

MR. DARWIN. Did this hum when it lighted?

ARCHIE. Yes, sir, it hummed when it lighted. (*Boys nod and whisper to each other,* "It hummed.")

MR. DARWIN. Now, think before you speak. Did this hum when you caught it?

ARCHIE. Yes, sir, it hummed when I caught it.

MR. DARWIN. Just as I thought. (*Puts glasses in pockets.*)

ARCHIE. What, sir?

MR. DARWIN (*wisely*). This hummed, and it hummed, and it hummed. (*All nod.*) It is a humbug! (*Hands mounting to* Archie.) Good day, sirs. (*Makes dignified exit.*)

(Archie's *mouth drops. He stands limp.*)

ARCHIE. A humbug. Mr. Darwin called this a humbug!

(Other Boys *laugh at* Archie *and repeat* "humbug!")

PERCY. I always said, "You can't fool Mr. Darwin."

(Boys *exit laughing saying* "Humbug." Archie *returns to table and picks up glue, tweezers, and so on, saying,* "Humbug! Bah, humbug!" *If there is no curtain, he exits in the opposite direction from* Other Boys.)

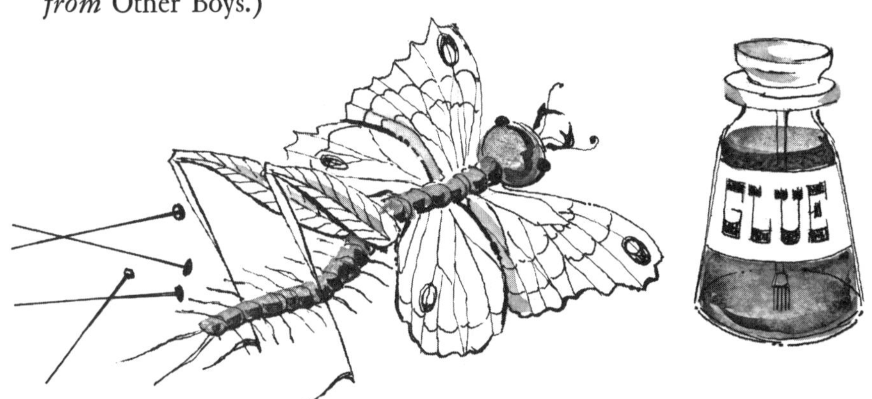

PLAY A PART

LET HER RIDE!

Introduction

This playlet gives a chance for some good acting as the busybody gossips nearly get into a street fight. You must present a tense moment without letting the situation on stage get out of control. Although the gossips may seem funny to the audience, actors must take their ridiculous attitudes seriously. Most of the characters gradually change their minds as William Penn reasons with them. The change must come slowly.

You may have as many characters as practical. If necessary, the crowd may be limited to five or six characters. The characters in the crowd may be all women, all men, or a combination of men, women, and children. The names are not important.

However, the historical personality of William Penn is important. His clear thinking, tolerance, and noble bearing must stand out in contrast to the conduct of the easily influenced mob. His punch line must be spoken slowly, clearly, loudly, and with authority.

This playlet is based on a true story. It may help to explain, in part, why colonial Pennsylvania escaped the "witch hunts" that resulted in the death of a number of old women in New England.

When a woman was accused of being a witch and brought before William Penn, he let her go, saying that nothing important had been proved against her. Tradition says that he added, in fun, "If she can ride through the air on a broomstick, let her ride."

Characters

Mrs. Harkins	Mrs. Hall
Mrs. Winters	Mr. Smith
Mrs. Foster	William Penn
Mr. Steiner	Other People

REAL-LIFE DRAMA

SCENE. *A street in Philadelphia in colonial times.* Mrs. Harkins *is sweeping the cobblestones in front of her home as people pass by, each saying,* "Good morning," *as she answers,* "Good morning," *or* "Nice day" *as she answers,* "Very nice day." *Some people stop to chat in small groups.* Mrs. Winters *enters, very excited.*

MRS. WINTERS. Mrs. Harkins! Mrs. Harkins! Have you heard the news? (*Everyone turns to listen.*)

MRS. HARKINS. News? What news? I have heard no news except—"It's a nice day."

MRS. WINTERS. No, no, no, no! Real news. Old Dame Dunniwell is a witch!

(*Members of crowd murmur* "witch" *and look at each other.*)

MRS. HARKINS. Dame Dunniwell a witch! Come now. What makes you think that Dame Dunniwell is a witch?

MRS. WINTERS. Well, I have suspected for a long time that she is a witch. Her and her queer ways. Living alone in that damp little cottage. (*Members of crowd agree.*)

MRS. HARKINS. Where else can she live? She has no kin. She's a burden to no one with her little garden. Excuse me. I have work to do. (*Resumes sweeping.*)

MRS. WINTERS. But you haven't heard the real news.

MRS. HARKINS. Then tell me.

MRS. WINTERS (*as crowd listens intently*). Last night when the moon was full, (*The speaker pauses dramatically to be sure she has the complete attention of the crowd.*) Samuel Ellis saw her ride through the air on a broomstick!

(*The crowd chatters:* "I saw something last night," "I knew she was a witch," *and so on. Above the chatter* Mrs. Harkins *speaks loudly and firmly.*)

MRS. HARKINS. Samuel Ellis saw a cloud—just a cloud.

MRS. WINTERS. No! No! That was no cloud. It was Dame Dunniwell riding through the air on a broomstick. Dame Dunniwell is a witch. I *know.*

MRS. FOSTER. I think she ought to be tried.

MR. HAMPTON. So do I. They burn witches in England.

MR. STEINER. In Germany, too.

MRS. WINTERS. And in New England.

MRS. HARKINS (*shouting*). Mrs. Winters. (*Others are quiet.*) May I remind you that Pennsylvania is not New England.

MRS. WINTERS. I know that Pennsylvania is not New England.

MRS. HARKINS. Then stop talking like a Yankee!

MRS. WINTERS. Yankee! She called me a Yankee. . . . I'll teach you to call me a Yankee. (*She tries to grab broomstick.*)

MRS. HARKINS. Then don't talk about burning old women as witches. (*They continue to tug on the broomstick and yell at each other. Crowd joins in the yelling as they pair off in groups of two or three, or try to pull the two women a part.* William Penn *enters.*)

PENN. Women, women, what is happening? (*Crowd is quiet.*) Do you not know that this is the City of Brotherly Love?

MRS. HARKINS. Brotherly love, sir? How can it be the City of Brotherly Love or sisterly love when Mrs. Winters accuses old Dame Dunniwell of being a witch?

PENN. A witch. What has she done?

MRS. HARKINS. Nothing.

MRS. WINTERS. She rode through the air on a broomstick.

OTHERS (*talking at once*). We saw her last night. She was bent over like this. She had a broom—

(Penn *motions for all to be quiet.*)

PENN. You say that Dame Dunniwell rode through the air on a broomstick. Therefore, she is a witch.

MRS. FOSTER. Yes, sir. We think the authorities should take action.

MRS. HALL. Dump her in water. See if she sinks.

MRS. FOSTER. Burn her, as they do in New England. (Penn *and* Mrs. Harkins *are horrified.*)

MRS. HARKINS. No, no! She's just an old woman.

MR. SMITH. We'll accept your decision, sir. Should Dame

Dunniwell be brought to trial? Will you give us an answer?

PENN. That's a serious question. You say that Dame Dunniwell is a witch.

MRS. HARKINS. No!

OTHERS. Aye!

MRS. WINTERS. We are convinced that Dame Dunniwell is a witch.

PENN. You say she rode through the air on a broomstick.

OTHERS. Aye!

MRS. HARKINS. It was a cloud.

PENN. This is the only evidence you wish to present against Dame Dunniwell. You say you saw her ride through the air on a broomstick. (*Crowd nods.*)

PENN. Let us consider the facts. One: are you sure that witches exist? (*Everyone talks at once excitedly.*)

MRS. HARKINS. No, they are just old women.

MRS. WINTERS. Aye, witches exist.

MRS. HALL. There're witches in New England.

MR. SMITH. And in Europe. (*Each makes a remark about witches.* Penn *raises his hand for quiet.*)

PENN. I see. Most of you believe in witches. (*Everyone except* Mrs. Harkins *nods.*) Question two: Are you sure that witches ride through the air on broomsticks?

MRS. HARKINS. No!

OTHERS. (*All talk at once.*) Aye. Witches ride through the air on broomsticks. We've seen them. Just last night—(Penn *raises his hand for quiet.*)

PENN. I see. Most of you believe that witches ride through the air on broomsticks. Now, tell me this: How does a witch harm a person by riding through the air on a broomstick. (*Crowd mumbles uncertainly.*)

MRS. HARKINS. I'd like to know the answer to that.

MRS. WINTERS. Well, a witch sets a bad example. It isn't ladylike to ride through the air on a broomstick. (*Most of the crowd nod their heads in agreement.*)

PENN. Do other women copy her?

MRS. WINTERS. Not unless they are witches.

PENN. Did you ever copy her? (*Then, pointing to other women.*) Or you? Or you? (*Pointing to* Mr. Smith.) Or your wife?

(Penn *paces slowly in deep thought as crowd waits eagerly for him to speak.*)

PENN. Personally, I do not believe in witches. I do not believe that anyone rides through the air on a broomstick. However, I could be wrong. (*Crowd is excited.* Penn *raises hand for quiet.*) For argument's sake, let us assume that there are witches. (*Crowd is happy.*) Let us assume that witches ride through the air on broomsticks. (*Crowd is delighted.*) One question remains unanswered: specifically, how does a witch harm anyone by riding through the air on a broomstick?

(*Members of crowd look at each other with a* "Don't know" *expression.*)

MR. SMITH. Sir, you've missed the real question. As I said before. We'll accept your decision. What are you going to do about Dame Dunniwell? What do you say?

PENN. Nothing important has been proved against Dame Dunniwell. I say, *"If* she can ride through the air on a broomstick, let her ride!" Good day. (*Exits. Crowd is amazed. When* Penn *has left the stage,* Mrs. Harkins *starts to laugh.*)

MRS. HARKINS. Ha! Ha! Ha! You got your answer. *"If* she can ride through the air on a broomstick. . ." (*Raises her broom high.*) "let her ride!" (*With broom still held high, she exits saying,* "Let her ride! Let her ride!"

MRS. WINTERS. I say Dame Dunniwell is a witch. She rides through the air on a broomstick. (*Stamps off stage.*)

MR. STEINER. As William Penn said, "What's the harm in riding?"

REMAINING CROWD. What harm? (*Gesture to each other as if saying,* " I don't know.")

MRS. SMITH. I have changed my mind. I stand behind William Penn: *If* she can ride through the air on a broomstick, let her ride.

OTHERS. Aye! Let her ride! Let her ride! (*If there is no curtain, actors exit saying,* "Let her ride! Let her ride!")

TO BUILD A FEDERAL CITY

Introduction

During the early years of American history a free Negro was often treated with respect. This was especially true when the Negro had marked ability, as was the case of Benjamin Banneker, surveyor, astronomer, and publisher of an almanac.

Beyond a doubt Benjamin Banneker was sometimes insulted because of his race; but he was also admired because of his intelligence, knowledge, skill, and eagerness to work beyond the call of duty. He shows, in this sketch, that although he is irritated by insults, he will not let an insulting attitude hinder him from contributing in a unique way to the development of the new country which he loves. He has faith in his own ability. Men who have worked with him are quick to testify to the quality of Banneker's ability.

Thomas Jefferson is known to have exhibited a hot temper when angry. He is very angry and worried as this sketch opens. Toward the close he is quick to express his thanks to Mr. Banneker and to other men who helped solve the problem facing the new government.

All of the other characters express concern about the problem and are eager to see it solved.

Two or more narrators, if available, will lend interest and provide a change of voices in giving the audience historical information.

PLAY A PART

Characters

THOMAS JEFFERSON, SECRETARY OF STATE
UNDERSECRETARY OF STATE
DANIEL CARROLL
MAJOR ANDREW ELLICOTT, Chief Surveyor
BENJAMIN BANNEKER, Negro Surveyor
MR. JONES, Surveyor
MR. SMITH, Surveyor
NARRATOR OR NARRATORS

SCENE. *A conference room, 1792. A long conference table is placed downstage. This may be any kind of table or a combination of tables large enough to seat five men along the side so they face the audience, and one man at each end. Chairs are placed in these positions. The table may be draped with any heavy cloth extending to the floor, like the conference tables at the colonial capitol at Williamsburg, Virginia.*

Chairs placed at the back of the table must be spaced in such a way that Jefferson *can step between them in the opening scene and lean over the table as he speaks.*

FIRST NARRATOR. Washington, D.C., the capital of the United States, is built according to a design prepared by a Frenchman, Pierre Charles L'Enfant. Little is ever said about the crisis that arose shortly before the city was established.

SECOND NARRATOR. President George Washington commissioned Mr. L'Enfant to survey the site chosen by Congress and make plans for the federal city. Mr. L'Enfant had grand plans. In his first year he spent more money than the entire sum allocated for the complete project. Congress decided to sell lots in the city to raise additional funds.

Mr. L'Enfant did not work well with people. He had to have his own way. No other way would do. He did not like the plan by which the lots were to be sold. Angry, he left for France, taking with him all the survey maps.

Third Narrator. Mr. Thomas Jefferson, who was then the Secretary of State, was in a spot. He had little to show for the money that had been spent, only the original sketch of the general plan. That was all. There was no survey plan of the lots to be sold. The date for sale of lots had been set. No one had a duplicate set of plans. There was neither money nor time to make a new survey. Let's see what happened.

(*As the scene opens,* Jefferson *is pacing the floor in a rage. His* Undersecretary *and* Carroll *are trying vainly to get his attention. After a short period of pantomime, the* Undersecretary *calls out.*)

Undersecretary. Mr. Secretary! Mr. Secretary! Mr. Thomas Jefferson, Secretary of State!

Jefferson. Well! What is it?

Undersecretary. Will you please calm down?

Carroll. Will you listen to reason?

Jefferson (*leaning over table*). Calm down? Listen to reason? Do you realize Charles L'Enfant has gone to France?

Carroll. You had to dismiss him, sir. He tore down my house, without yes or no. You had to dismiss him.

Undersecretary. He was above authority, sir. You had to dismiss him.

Jefferson (*slowly*). Pierre L'Enfant went to France *before* he was dismissed. Before he received terms of dismissal.

Carroll and Undersecretary. Well—

Jefferson. He took with him the survey plans of the federal city of Washington.

Carroll and Undersecretary. No!

Jefferson. We have nothing to show for all the money the government has spent on surveys.

Undersecretary. There's the original plan.

Jefferson. A sketch, more or less. There is no record of the survey.

Carroll. The sale of lots? The date has been set.

Jefferson. Yes, the date for the sale of lots has been set. We have no records of the lots.

UNDERSECRETARY. Well, I'm glad I asked Major Ellicott to come here.

CARROLL. Major Andrew Ellicott, in charge of the survey?

UNDERSECRETARY. Yes, he is waiting now.

JEFFERSON. Waiting? Why didn't you tell me?

UNDERSECRETARY. I was trying, sir. Excuse me. (*Exits.*)

CARROLL. Indeed, sir, we were both trying to tell you.

(Mr. Undersecretary *returns with* Major Ellicott, Banneker, *and two other surveyors.*)

JEFFERSON (*stepping forward*). Major Ellicott.

MAJOR ELLICOTT. May I present my surveyors, Mr. Jones, Mr. Smith, Mr. Banneker.

(Jefferson *introduces the other men. Greetings are exchanged quickly.*)

JEFFERSON. Please be seated.

(Jefferson *sits in the center chair with his* Undersecretary *on his right, and* Carroll *next to him.* Ellicott *sits on* Jefferson's *left with* Banneker *next to him.* Smith *and* Jones *sit at the ends of the table.*)

JEFFERSON. Major Ellicott, gentlemen, may I bring you up to date on the project of our federal city of Washington in the territory of Columbia. To put it bluntly, Pierre Charles L'Enfant, the planner, has gone to France, taking with him all of the survey maps.

ELLICOTT AND SURVEYORS. No.

JEFFERSON. Does anyone have a copy of the survey maps?

MAJOR ELLICOTT. No, sir, Mr. L'Enfant would let no one copy his maps. He feared land speculation, or so he said.

SMITH. When I handed in my data, he wouldn't let me see a thing.

JONES. He wouldn't let anyone work with him on drawings except Benjamin Banneker.

JEFFERSON. Mr. Banneker, do you have duplicate drawings?

BANNEKER. Duplicate drawings, Mr. Jefferson? You mean—

Would Mr. L'Enfant let *me* make duplicate drawings? (*Pauses and smiles.*) I don't know quite how to say it, but Mr. L'Enfant always treated me like a houseboy—unless he wanted to know something he should have known himself.

ELLICOTT. Don't take offense, Mr. Banneker. Mr. L'Enfant treated everyone like a houseboy: Mr. Washington, Mr. Jefferson, the commissioners, and especially the surveyors, including me. We all know that you are an excellent surveyor.

JEFFERSON. Gentlemen! Gentlemen! Please let's not discuss Mr. L'Enfant, a brilliant dreamer who envisioned a beautiful city and an impractical man who would work with no one. The question is: What can we do now? We have no survey plans. Major Ellicott, what is your opinion?

ELLICOTT. I think, sir, the only thing to do is to make a new survey.

JEFFERSON, CARROLL, UNDERSECRETARY. Impossible!

JEFFERSON (*clearly and heatedly*). Major Ellicott, may I remind you that surveys take time and money. We have already exceeded our budget by a million dollars. We have no money. We have no time. The only way to get money is to sell lots. The date for the sale of lots is set, and we have no survey plans of the lots. (*Silence.*) Does anyone have a plan?

BANNEKER. Mr. Jefferson, I could draw those plans for you.

JEFFERSON. Draw the plans? Then you do have a copy?

BANNEKER. No, sir. I have the plans in my head.

JEFFERSON. You mean, you could draw the plans from memory?

BANNEKER. Yes, I could.

JEFFERSON. Incredible! How long do you think it would take?

BANNEKER. Three days, at the most, sir. (Jefferson *hesitates.*)

ELLICOTT. I'm sure he can do it, sir. He has a remarkable memory.

SMITH. He's a great worker, sir.

JONES. He never brags, sir. Just goes ahead.

CARROLL. What can you lose?

UNDERSECRETARY. Let him try.

JEFFERSON (*standing*). Mr. Benjamin Banneker, I commission you to deliver to Major Ellicott in as short a time as practical, survey plans for the federal city, to be called the city of Washington in the territory of Columbia.

Major Ellicott, upon receipt of these plans you will deliver them

to me and the commissioners for examination and, if necessary, revision. Then Major Ellicott, you will prepare the plans for engraving with due speed.

MAJOR ELLICOTT. Yes, sir.

BANNEKER (*rising*). Thank you, sir. You shall have your plans. (*Lifts hands.*) These hands will draw your plans. These hands will help to build a federal city. Good-bye, Mr. Secretary. Good-bye, gentlemen. (*Other men rise to nod* "Good-bye.")

JEFFERSON. Good-bye, Mr. Banneker, and Godspeed! (Banneker *exits.*)

JEFFERSON (*musing*). Godspeed and thank you. (*Raises voice.*) Gentlemen, I truly believe that, thanks in great part to Mr. Benjamin Banneker, we shall have in good speed our federal city of Washington. (*Others nod.*)

ANOTHER WAY

(The Mayflower Compact)

Introduction

Edward Dotey and Edward Leister in this dramatic scene are very much like braggarts everywhere: loudmouthed and quick to fight when showing off; scared stiff when someone calls their bluff and reveals their plans. They and other indentured servants on the Mayflower are unable to grasp the meaning of the Mayflower Compact whereby each man pledges to work for "the general good of the colony." They are willing, however, to sign if asked. Any arrangement seems better than being hung for mutiny.

Christopher Jones, captain of the Mayflower represents authority. He didn't pretend to understand the Pilgrims; but he did admire them in a certain way, and he did help them even when his sailors complained.

History hints at proposed mutiny on the Mayflower. We do not know that Captain Jones helped to break the mutineers' plans, but he might have. He would play his role in this scene with dignity and a certain quiet enjoyment of seeing men squirm when caught in evil planning.

Captain Jones realizes that the Mayflower Compact is a very unusual document. He speaks of it and its authors with respect. He makes the audience appreciate its importance.

(If you wish you can omit the closing comment by the narrator and enact the signing of the Mayflower Company. Many encyclopedias and history books include the exact words of the compact.

No doubt the Mayflower Compact was read aloud by John Carver. Group men and women with Carver standing behind a small table at center stage. Let Captain Jones call out the names as each person signs. Dotey and Leister are in line, toward its end. Lower the curtain as names are read, starting in this order: John Carver, William Bradford, Edward Winslow, William Brewster, Isaac Allerton, Miles Standish, Samuel Fuller, William White—)

Characters

EDWARD DOTEY } Indentured Servants
EDWARD LEISTER } of Stephen Hopkins

OTHER SERVANTS (*up to sixteen*)

CAPTAIN JONES

NARRATOR

SCENE. *Crowded servants' quarters on the Mayflower.*

NARRATOR. Pilgrim leaders faced a desperate situation when at last they sighted land. Christopher Jones, captain of the Mayflower, informed them that the land was not in Virginia Colony, where they had planned to settle. It was in Plymouth Plantation. Captain Jones advised them, and they agreed, this was the spot where they must land and settle, because winter was at hand.

Fine legal points arose. What authority, if any, did the Pilgrims have in land not covered by their charter? If they had no authority in this land, were their servants still indentured?

Thoughts went back to 1609 when a ship headed for Virginia was shipwrecked off Bermuda. Landing on shore, a group of mutineers felt they were automatically "freed from the government of any man." The mutiny ended by the hanging of the men involved. Only one man was spared, Stephen Hopkins.

Pilgrim leaders feared that indentured servants on the Mayflower might mutiny as soon as they set foot on land not covered by the charter. Although he did not mention the malcontents by name, William Bradford wrote in his history, "Some were not affected to unity and concord; but gave some appearance of faction."

How did the Pilgrim leaders prevent mutiny? Let's see what might have happened on the Mayflower.

(Leister *and another servant are seated at a very small table, center stage, engaged in hand wrestling, or other physical contest that can be done in a small space.* Other servants *are watching and cheering favorites. They laugh lustily when one is pushed down.* Dotey *rushes in.*)

DOTEY. It's true! It's true!

OTHERS. What's true? Tell us.

DOTEY. We're not landing in Virginia.

LEISTER. Where are we landing?

DOTEY. Cape Cod. We're landing at Cape Cod.

OTHERS. So—

DOTEY. Cape Cod's in Plymouth Plantation.

FIRST SERVANT. What does that mean?

LEISTER. Don't you know?

DOTEY. Don't any of you know?

OTHERS. No.

DOTEY. The Virginia patent doesn't cover Plymouth Plantation.

FIRST SERVANT. No patent?

DOTEY. No patent and no masters!

SECOND SERVANT. We're indentured. Under English law, we are indentured.

DOTEY. Under English law, the sober-sided saints have no rights in Plymouth Plantation. (*Enter* Captain Jones, *unseen.*) When we set foot on Plymouth soil, we'll mutiny.

LEISTER. Like they did in Jamestown, 1609.

FIRST SERVANT. Jamestown, 1609? They were hung. Those that mutinied were hung, except Stephen Hopkins.

DOTEY. Stephen Hopkins, my worthy master. (*Points to* Leister.) I should say, our worthy master. This time will be different. Leister and I have planned it.

LEISTER. We've talked it over.

DOTEY. As soon as we land, I'll be in command.

LEISTER (*jumping up*). You'll be in command? I'll be in command!

(Dotey *walks slowly downstage where he confronts* Leister.)

DOTEY. Let's get this straight. I'll be in command.

LEISTER. I challenge you. (*They are posed for a fight when* Captain Jones *speaks.*)

CAPTAIN JONES. Dotey! Leister!

OTHERS. Captain Jones! (Captain Jones *steps between the two fighters.*)

CAPTAIN JONES. May I remind you, I am in command. As long as you are on my ship, I am in command.

DOTEY AND LEISTER. Aye, sir.

CAPTAIN JONES. I have come with a message from Master Carver.

LEISTER (*fearfully*). They know about it? (Servants *show panic.*)

DOTEY. What will they do?

CAPTAIN JONES. What do you think?

FIRST SERVANT. They could flog us all. We're here together.

JONES. Aye, they could flog you all.

SECOND SERVANT. Or cut off our ears. We're all listening.

JONES. They could cut off your ears. It's been done before for less reason.

DOTEY. They could hang us.

LEISTER. Like Jamestown, 1609.

JONES. Yes, the leaders could be hung for mutinous intentions.

(Dotey *and* Leister *fall on knees and beg for mercy.*)

DOTEY AND LEISTER. No! No! Mercy! Have mercy!

CAPTAIN JONES. The saints are filled with mercy and good sense. (*There is silence as everyone waits for* Captain Jones's *next words.*) They do not plan to hang or mutilate able-bodied people. God knows, and the saints know, that they need the help of every able-bodied person to settle this wild land. The saints have found a new way to smother mutiny.

(Dotey *and* Leister *rise, still awed.*)

DOTEY. A new way?

JONES. They plan to bind together saints, strangers, servants, children—everyone—in a "body politic."

ALL (*confused*). A body politic?

JONES. Yes, you may recall that in his farewell letter to the Leyden group, Pastor Robinson charged them all to become a body politic. They tell me that members of the Church of Leyden have lived under a covenant for more than twelve years.

DOTEY (*relieved*). So that's it. Covenant. We pledge to the Covenant. No noose! (*Others are in joyful mood.*)

JONES. No, that's not it. This is something new. Something written by Master William Brewster and Master Stephen Hopkins.

DOTEY. My master.

LEISTER. We may hang yet.

JONES. This compact is the Mayflower Compact.

OTHERS. Mayflower Compact. What's that?

JONES. It is a pledge for all to work for the general good of the colony.

DOTEY. All to work for the general good. You mean—I have to work for everyone—not just my master.

LEISTER. You mean my master has to work for others in the colony.

JONES. Exactly. Everyone works for the general good of the colony. Dotey, Leister, I advise you to sign the compact, if you are asked to do so.

DOTEY. I'm still indentured.

LEISTER. Can an indentured servant sign?

JONES. For the first time in history, as far as I know, every man, regardless of his rank, will be asked to sign a compact, pledging himself to work for the general good of everyone.

(Servants *shake heads, unable to understand.*)

JONES. I advise you, everyone. Erase all mutiny from your hearts. Sign the Mayflower Compact.

NARRATOR. Before disembarking from the Mayflower, members of the Pilgrim band assembled. Leaders read aloud the Mayflower Compact. Forty-one of the sixty-five males aboard signed the compact. Thirteen of those who did not sign were sons of signers, covered by their fathers' signatures. Nine servants and two hired sailors did not sign. They may have been too ill. Among the names of indentured servants who did sign we find two that interest us: Edward Leister and Edward Dotey.

There was no mutiny, no hanging of discontented passengers. A new rule was established in a new land. One small step toward democracy was taken when Pilgrim men of different classes signed the Mayflower Compact and pledged themselves to work for the general good of the colony.

REAL-LIFE DRAMA

REMEMBER THE CHRISTMAS TREE

Introduction

When enacting a scene from the Revolutionary War, it must be remembered that in many ways that war was a civil war, a war between colonists who wanted to remain faithful to England and colonists who felt it was necessary to form a new nation. In this scene the Hunts, the Potts, and their guests, like many other people living in New Jersey in 1776, consider themselves to be good English citizens. They are delighted to play host to the Hessian commandant, Colonel Johann Gottlieb Rall. As the play progresses, these people begin to wonder if the British and their Hessian allies are right and the Continentals wrong.

At the beginning of the scene Colonel Rall is a self-assured professional soldier, irritated by anyone who questions his opinion. In the closing scene, admitting his mistake takes courage.

The farmer has the dramatic part of a man who risks his very life to give information that is not wanted.

The opening scene must be very lively and gay, a great contrast from the final tragic scene. But even in the tragedy there is something beautiful: the hope that the scars of war will someday be forgotten and the beginning of an American tradition—the Hessian Christmas tree. Legend tells us that the Christmas tree originated in Germany; no doubt the Hessian soldiers conscripted by King George III brought with them and shared with the Colonists many pleasant memories of this lovely tradition.

Characters

COL. JOHANN GOTTLIEB RALL, Hessian commandant
ABRAHAM HUNT, Tory
MRS. HUNT
STACY POTTS, Tory
CAROLERS
MRS. POTTS
FARMER
NETTIE, a maid
OTHER GUESTS

SCENE I. *Home of* Mr. and Mrs. Abraham Hunt, *Trenton, New*

Jersey, December 25, 1776. A small table is placed downstage center with chairs grouped around the sides and in back. Other furniture may be placed around the room. An unlighted Christmas tree decorated with cooky cut-outs or other old-fashioned ornaments stands at back, left.

The Hunts *and their guests are gathered around the table, gaily singing and drinking toasts to* Colonel Rall, *the guest of honor. A group offstage is singing the familiar carol,* "O Christmas Tree." Mrs. Hunt *goes to door.*

MRS. HUNT. Come in! Come in! (Carolers *enter singing, mingling with guests who also sing.*)

CAROLERS. O Christmas Tree, O Christmas Tree,
How faithful are thy branches!
O Christmas Tree, O Christmas Tree,
How faithful are thy branches!
Green not alone in Summer time;
But in the Winter's frost and rune;
O Christmas Tree, O Christmas Tree,
How lovely are thy branches!

'Tis not alone in Summer's sheen,
Its boughs are broad, its leaves are green;
It blooms for us when wild winds blow,
And earth is white with feath'ry snow;
A voice tells all its boughs among
Of shepherd's watch and angel's song;
Of holy Babe in manger low,
The story of so long ago.

HUNTS AND GUESTS. Thank you. Thank you.

LEADER OF CAROLERS. Merry Christmas to you. We must go. (*Exit singing,* "O Christmas Tree, etc." *Others are humming with them.*)

MRS. HUNT. "O Christmas Tree." That's a lively song.

MRS. POTTS. The very spirit of Christmas.

MR. HUNT. A toast to the Christmas tree.

MRS. HUNT. And to the Hessian soldiers who gave us the Christmas tree!

MR. POTTS. And to Colonel Rall, who leads the Hessians!

COLONEL RALL. Thank you! Thank you! And now a toast to the British in America. May you win this war of insurrection and spend every Christmas in a jolly place like this.

ALL. To the British!

MRS. HUNT. Tell us, Colonel Rall, has your day been pleasant?

COLONEL RALL (*changing mood*). Pleasant? With a storm raging outside? Cold and bitter, blast New Jersey weather!

MR. POTTS. You must admit, sir. The storm keeps Washington holed up at Valley Forge, across the Delaware. (*Ladies are seated.*)

COLONEL RALL. Holed up. That's a good term. Holed-up just like an animal in his winter den. And mark my words, Washington will not leave that den 'til spring. (*Others nod as* Rall *sips.*) At least Washington cannot cross the Delaware tonight.

MR. POTTS. Who doubts that, sir?

COLONEL RALL. Who doubts it? Let me tell you what my day has been. Or let me start with last night, Christmas Eve. (*Sits right of table.*) At exactly 11 p.m., His Honor, Maj. Gen. James Grant, commander of the Fourth British Brigade at Prince Town, took it upon himself to write me a note. (*Mimics the British officer.*) "Be upon your guard against an unexpected attack on Trenton."

MRS. POTTS. General Grant is a fuss-budget.

MR. POTTS (*mimicking self-assured general*). Always proper. Always right. Very British, don't you know?

COLONEL RALL. Dawn broke, gray and cold. In came a junior officer. "Sir," he asks, "don't you think we should hide the baggage in case of sudden attack?"

MR. HUNT. What did you say, sir?

COLONEL RALL. "If they come, all they can hope for is a sudden retreat."

OTHERS. Well said!

MR. POTTS. A professional outlook!

COLONEL RALL. However, I checked the guards, listened to more dismal rumors, and then celebrated Christmas in a fitting manner. I played checkers with my good friend Stacy Potts. (Mr. Potts *smiles.*)

OTHERS. Good.

MRS. HUNT. Did you win?

MR. POTTS. No time to win. At 7 p.m. our game was interrupted by shooting.

OTHERS. What was it?

COLONEL RALL. Farmers. Farmers taking potshots at the Hessian outposts, just for Christmas fun. (Nettie *enters with a tray of food.*)

MRS. HUNT. Farmers trying to be soldiers! Come, let us eat. (*Loud knocking is heard on door.*)

FARMER (*calling from outside*). Colonel Rall! Colonel Rall!

MRS. HUNT. Who can that be? Nettie, run to the door!

FARMER. I must talk to Colonel Rall!

MRS. HUNT. Colonel Rall is busy.

FARMER (*dashing in front of others*). Sir, I have crossed the Delaware. I have come to warn you!

COLONEL RALL (*rising*). Sir, I think you are numb with cold.

FARMER (*interrupting*). You must listen. (*Coughs.*) Washington plans to cross the Delaware tonight with 2,400 men. (*Coughs.*) They started to assemble, at 3 p.m.—outside the ferry house. (*Coughs.*)

COLONEL RALL. There, there! You are exhausted, and so am I. All day long I have heard rumors. I have checked them all.

FARMER. Sir, here are the plans. Everything on paper. (*Hands paper to* Rall *who stiffens as he clenches the paper in his fist.*)

COLONEL RALL. Plans? You mean rumors. Rumors on paper. Rumors on tongues. Rumors! Rumors! Rumors! I am tired of rumors!

(*Others are stunned.* Mrs. Hunt *tries to lead* Farmer *into kitchen as* Rall *rages.*)

Mrs. Hunt. Come, let me help you.

Farmer. No, No. If you won't listen, I must find someone else. I must warn someone. Washington is crossing the Delaware! (*He dashes out of the door. Some follow the farmer to the door. Then gather at center stage.*)

Mrs. Hunt. Poor man!

Mrs. Potts. Frozen, half-out of his wits.

(Rall *deliberately jams paper into his pocket without reading it. Stiffens.*)

Colonel Rall (*angrily*). The next self-appointed informant who tells me, a professional officer, that Washington plans to cross the Delaware tonight will—

Mr. Potts. Have you checked the Delaware, sir?

Colonel Rall. Sir, do you question my professional judgment? (*Silence.*) The Delaware is on a rampage. The current is raging. The ice is increasing. The wind is raw. No one—no one can cross the Delaware tonight.

Mr. Hunt. The farmer, sir. He does not live near Trenton.

Colonel Rall (*standing very straight and speaking slowly.*) In my professional opinion no one can cross the Delaware tonight with 2,400 troops. No one. Not even Washington! (*Silence.*) Ladies— (*Bows.*) Gentlemen— (*Bows.*) Good night. (*There is dead silence as* Mr. Hunt *escorts* Colonel Rall *to the door.* Mr. Hunt *returns to center stage.*)

Mr. Hunt (*musing*). Good night. Is this night so very good for Tories and the British?

Mr. Potts. I'm not sure.

Mr. Hunt. Nor am I.

(Mrs. Potts *stands next to* Mr. Potts, *and* Mrs. Hunt *next to* Mr. Hunt.)

Mrs. Hunt. Oh, cheer up! It's Christmas night. The tree is pretty—our first Christmas tree.

Mrs. Potts. Yes, why should we worry? Remember: in the professional opinion of Colonel Rall, Washington cannot cross the Delaware tonight!

(Curtain)

Scene II. *Home of* Mr. *and* Mrs. Stacy Potts *after the battle. Furniture may be the same, but rearranged a little.* Colonel Rall *sits left stage, wounded.* Mrs. Potts *stands behind him, bathing his head.* Mr. Potts *is seated near table right.*)

Colonel Rall. How could he? How could he?

Mr. Potts. Please, be quiet, sir. You are wounded.

Colonel Rall. Wounded? I am dying. The ghost of Washington stands before me. I can see him, and his 2,400 ragtag men, appearing like ghosts out of the fog. (*Pauses.*) Nine hundred and eighteen Hessians killed, wounded, or captured. Four Americans wounded.

Mr. Potts (*rising*). Pull yourself together, sir. General Washington will be here soon.

Colonel Rall. Washington here? In person?

Mr. Potts. Yes, sir. I have been told he will offer you parole.

Colonel Rall. And my men?

MR. POTTS. He has promised to treat them kindly.

COLONEL RALL. Generous. Washington is generous, brave, and daring. Oh, my leg. (*Feels thigh.*) Oh, the paper. (*He pulls paper from his pocket. Opens it. Reads to himself.*) It's here. All here. Every detail. (*Drops hand with paper in his lap.*) If I had read this last night, I wouldn't be here today.

(Mrs. Potts *steps a little center stage and puts her left hand on his shoulder.*)

MRS. POTTS. There, there.

COLONEL RALL. Thank you, Mrs. Potts, and Mr. Potts. Thank you for your kindness. Try to forget the Hessians.

MRS. POTTS. Not the Hessians. Someday, no matter what happens, we'll try to forget the war. But we shall always remember the Hessians and their Christmas tree.

COLONEL RALL. Good, good. Remember the Christmas tree. Forget the stubbornness of Colonel Rall. (*He muses.*) How could he do it? How could General George Washington cross the Delaware with 2,400 men on a night like that?

(Curtain)

HBC
FORT HALL
HUDSONS BAY COMPANY

PLAYS

In a play, actors present a dramatized record of a struggle. In order to appreciate the play the audience must understand the problem, must know why a conflict arose or what caused the problem, and must find out what happens. If the production is to be successful, the audience must learn to know as individuals the people involved in the play, and thus be able to understand why each character reacts as he does.

To be able to fulfill their duty to the audience, the cast must understand the play and the people in it. Each actor must develop insight into the character he portrays. (See pages 13-19.) He must also understand the role of other characters in the play.

A play has three main parts—introduction, body, and climax. Each actor must understand how each part of the play contributes to the success of the entire production.

In the introduction, that is, in the first part of the play, the actors must do four things: (1) gain the attention of the audience and arouse interest; (2) establish the atmosphere of the play; (3) give necessary background information; and, (4) introduce principal characters. (A principal character does not have to be in the introductory portion of the scene, but the audience must understand his importance early in the play.)

The opening scene of a play is much like the topic sentence of a good lecture. If carefully planned, it attracts and holds the attention of the audience.

The author of a play plans the opening scene, but the actors must determine its role and fulfill it. For example, if the scene opens with pantomime, that is, with one or more actors pretending to do something—read a book, arrange flowers in a vase, look for something, or clean a window—the actor must determine how long to continue to pantomime before speaking himself or before some other character speaks. If a play opens with casual conversation, the actors must know what points in the conversation are important. If the scene opens with a loud noise, the appearance of an unusual character, or some other device, the actors in their response to this opening device must produce the desired effect upon the audience.

Scenery may help to produce atmosphere, but the actors' reactions are vital. A bare stage may become spooky if actors are capable of making the audience feel that the place is inhabited by ghosts.

There are several ways to introduce characters and give background information. Shakespeare sometimes had a servant, or some other character, step before the audience and tell who the characters would be, what had happened before the opening scene, and what to expect. This device still is used on occasion. As a rule, a situation is discussed by characters in the play. Pinpointing lines and getting them across to the audience is extremely important.

In the body of the play the plot is developed. Interest must not lag. All actors must remain constantly alert. They must know their lines so well that they think in terms of ideas, not words. A slight mistake in a cue will not upset an actor who is familiar with all the lines and who does not depend on a single word or phrase as a cue.

At last the play comes to a climax, the point of highest tension. Everything that has been said or done in the introduction and in the body of the play has led to this moment, which must be highly dramatic.

The principal character should have the center of the stage. If he is speaking, he should stand or sit front center. If he is about to exit upstage center the stage in front of him should be bare. All attention must be focused on the principal character in the climactic moment.

The play may end with the climax or it may end with the actors reacting to the climax. For example, after hearing certain news they may cheer, sing, or mourn as the situation demands. The play will have a triumphant ending if each actor—major or minor—plays his part from beginning to end.

GHOSTS

Introduction

A ghost play can be given any time of year. Most of the ghosts in this skit express their emotions by saying "Oooh—" or "Booo!" in different ways. They must control the volume so that other players can speak and be heard above their groans. If speakers wait until the ghosts have completed each groan, the skit will drag.

The speaking ghosts must get their punch lines across: "Once a Texan, always a Texan"; "Texans tell tall tales"; and "A ghost can't live it up." Of course, these lines are also important when said by other characters.

Mike and Molly, as an American boy and girl from Texas, bubble with excitement and enthusiasm at the idea of ghosts and sink into deep despair when they realize that the ghosts have disappeared and no one will believe their tall-tale experience of dancing the Irish jig with Irish ghosts. Having someone play an Irish jig on a violin or accordion would be effective and make timing easy. However, offstage music can be used.

Mr. and Mrs. Terwinkle are practical Americans, set for new experiences and even new adventures if they are to be found. Their common sense and past experience, however, lead them to recognize a tall tale when they hear it. Or at least that's what they think!

Avoid using masks for ghosts with speaking parts. If possible, use theatrical makeup and paint the ghosts' faces white. If you do use masks, choose the half-face kind and make sure that eyes are properly placed and large enough to allow each ghosts to see where he is going.

This skit can be given almost any place: at camp with woods or rocks for a background, at a club meeting with no curtain and a level floor. for a stage, or in a school auditorium. You can have as few as two ghosts or as many as you wish, providing that there is room for them to dance the Irish jig. The children may be two boys, or two girls, or a boy and a girl as in the script.

If the skit is produced on a stage without a curtain, for example, at a camp where ghosts go behind trees or rocks, the family will need exit lines. Mr. Terwinkle can say, "Let's get things settled" and can pick up some of the luggage. He will be followed offstage by Mrs. Terwinkle, also carrying luggage, and the children talking and doing the Irish jig as they carry off luggage.

The skit must have a spooky start, but it must not drag. Ghosts dancing the Irish jig should be very funny.

Characters

LORD TERENCE, ghost of Castle O'Toole	HENRY TERWINKLE, Texan
LADY GRANIA, his ghostly wife	MAUDE TERWINKLE, his wife
ONE KIN, another ghost	MOLLY TERWINKLE, their daughter
	MIKE TERWINKLE, their son

OTHER GHOSTS

SCENE. *Great hall of Castle O'Toole, an Irish castle deserted for four hundred years. Furniture is covered with sheets. At center stage is a couch with pillows on it. Nearby is a small table with a rag on it. Rag and pillows are covered with talcum powder that will look like clouds of dust when rag and pillows are shaken.*

There are three exits. Upstage center is a closet door, or a space in backdrop drapes through which ghosts enter and exit. Left front exit leads to outdoors. Right front exit leads to other rooms in the castle.

As the scene opens, Lord Terence, *wearing a coronet, is summoning the ghosts of the castle with loud wails. First to enter is* Lady Grania, *also wearing a coronet. Others follow. Each time* Lord Terence *speaks, the other ghosts nod or shake their heads and wail softly; but the wails must not drown out the speech of* Lady Grania.

LORD TERENCE. Owwww— Owww— Owwww—

OTHER GHOSTS (*entering*). Owww— Owww— Owww— (Lord Terence *and* Lady Grania *meet downstage center.*)

LADY GRANIA. My Lord Terence, why have you summoned us today?

LORD TERENCE. Some Texans are coming.

OTHER GHOSTS. Owww—

LADY GRANIA. Pray tell, what are Texans?

LORD TERENCE. A kind of American.

OTHER GHOSTS. Owww—

LADY GRANIA. An American is an American. What is special about a Texan?

LORD TERENCE. I have heard: "Once a Texan, always a Texan."

OTHER GHOSTS. Owww—

LADY GRANIA. What do you mean by that?

LORD TERENCE. A Texan tells tall tales.

OTHER GHOSTS. Owww—

LADY GRANIA. Oh, is that all? They tell tall tales. Let me remind you, Lord Terence O'Toole, ghosts tell the tallest tales. And Irish ghosts tell the tallest, tallest, tallest tales! (*Other ghosts, including* Lord Terence, *nod approval.*) For four hundred years we have kept people out of Castle O'Toole. (*Others nod agreement.*) How? By telling tall ghost tales. Everyone is afraid of ghosts!

LORD TERENCE. Texans are afraid of no one and no thing!

LADY GRANIA. Now, that's the tallest tale of all! We'll scare the living daylights out of the Texans. (*Turns to other ghosts.*) Won't we, kith and kin? (*Ghosts nod with low* "Owww—")

KIN. We'll scare the living daylights out of them. Then they'll be ghosts. Ha! Ha! Ha! (*Other ghosts nod and laugh.*)

LORD TERENCE (*bowing*). My dear Lady Grania, you are right. Without their living daylights, the Texans will be ghosts.

(*Offstage voices are heard.*)

MIKE. Here we are.

MR. TERWINKLE. The Castle O'Toole!

LORD TERENCE. Here they come. Remember! We'll scare the living daylights out of them. Then they'll be ghosts!

(*Ghosts howl softly and happily as they quickly exit upstage center.* Terwinkles *keep talking,* "Glad we got here," *and so on. Last ghost has to hurry to get out as* Terwinkles *enter, loaded down with luggage, cameras, and so on. If the last ghost doesn't get out,* Terwinkles *pay no attention, just cross stage, looking at ceiling, and so on.*)

MRS. TERWINKLE. Oh, Henry, it's just like you said, "Big, and old, and really antique." What more could a Texan want?

MIKE. And spooky, too.

MOLLY. Do you think we'll see ghosts?

MR. TERWINKLE. Sure, why not? The agents said ghosts haunt the place.

MIKE. Hope that's true. Wait 'til we write the kids, "We've got a castle with real ghosts."

MOLLY. They won't believe us.

MRS. TERWINKLE. They'll say, "Once a Texan, always a Texan."

MIKE. What's wrong with that?

MRS. TERWINKLE. Well, we Texans do have a reputation for telling tall tales. Now a ghost tale— (*She is interrupted by banging noise offstage.*)

MRS. TERWINKLE. What's that?

MR. TERWINKLE. Can't be the plumbing or the furnace.

MIKE (*happily*). Maybe it's a ghost clanking chains!

MR. TERWINKLE. I doubt it, but I'll see. (*Starts to cross right.*)

MRS. TERWINKLE. I thought it came from that way.

MR. TERWINKLE. That's right. No basement. Outside dungeon entrance. (*Exits left.* Mrs. Terwinkle *rubs finger on dusty table.*)

MRS. TERWINKLE. My goodness! Things certainly do get dusty in four hundred years! (*She picks up rag on table. Clouds of dust go into air.*)

MOLLY. You said it, Mom!

MRS. TERWINKLE. I'm going to look in the closets.

MIKE. For ghosts?

MRS. TERWINKLE. No! For mops and pails, and things to clean up this place.

MOLLY. Clean up this place? Once a Texan, always a Texan. (Mrs. Terwinkle *exits right.*)

MIKE. Dad rented a castle with ghosts. Now, I'm going to find the ghosts.

MOLLY. Me too. (*They get down on all fours and look under*

sofa. Ghosts enter saying "Owww—" Molly *and* Mike *pay no attention to them.* Molly *still on knees turns to* Mike.)

MOLLY. Mike, are you hungry?

MIKE. I'm always hungry. Why?

MOLLY. I thought I heard your stomach growling. (*Ghosts are disgusted. Howl again as children again look under sofa.*)

MIKE. Molly, are you hungry?

MOLLY. No, really. Why?

MIKE. I thought I heard your stomach growling.

(*Disappointed,* Mike *and* Molly *sit on sofa without noticing ghosts. Ghosts creep up behind them, with hands uplifted in frightening way. At signal from* Lord Terence, *they all yell.*)

GHOSTS. Boo! (Molly *and* Mike *look around delighted.*)

MOLLY. Look! Ghosts!

MIKE. Say, we were looking for you.

GHOSTS (*screaming*). Owwww—

MOLLY. Noisy creatures.

MIKE. Worse than coyotes. (Lord Terence *has come around so that he stands near* Molly, *and* Lady Grania *stands near* Mike. *They and other ghosts are as frightening as possible.* Mike *stands.*)

MIKE. Sorry I was impolite. I'm Mike Terwinkle. That's short for Michael Terwinkle. You must be Lord Terence O'Toole. (Molly *stands.*)

MOLLY. I'm Molly Terwinkle. That's short for Mary Martha Terwinkle. You must be Lady Grania O'Toole.

(Lady Grania *turns away disappointed that she hasn't scared* Mike *and* Molly. *She weeps* "Booo—" *Other ghosts cry with her.*)

MIKE. We're from Texas. (*Ghosts nod that they know.*) Our folks rented this spread for the summer. (*Ghosts nod.*) They aren't here just now.

MOLLY. So make yourselves at home. (*Ghosts pantomime,* "Us? Here? At home?") Come to think of it, you are at home. You've been here four hundred years.

MIKE. Sorry you don't like the place. We do. (Molly *agrees.*) So ghosts, let's stop moping around half-dead. What would you like to do? (*Ghosts pantomime* "Do?" *Some make motion to float through air.*)

MOLLY. No, we can't float. How about a pillow fight? (*Picks up pillow. Chokes on cloud of dust.*) Air pollution! Four hundred years of air pollution. (*Ghosts choke with moans.*)

MIKE. Let's box. You know, shadowbox. (*Holds up fists.*)

MOLLY. Hold it, Mike. You haven't got a ghost of a chance. Let's think of something lively.

MIKE (*discouraged*). Yeah. Something old, something dead, and something lively.

MOLLY. How about an Irish jig?

MIKE. I don't know an Irish jig.

MOLLY. That's it. It's so old, it's dead. At least we don't know it. I've heard it's lively. (*Ghosts nod.*) Let's ask the ghosts to teach us an Irish jig. (*Ghosts are shaking with excitement and making queer noises. Irish jig music is heard offstage, or a ghost picks up a violin or accordion.*) Hey, Mike, that must be an Irish jig coming back from the past!

(Lord Terence *beckons* Molly *to be his partner.* Lady Grania *chooses* Mike. *At a signal from* Lord Terence, *all dance an Irish jig. At end all are limp, and it is quiet.*)

MIKE. That was great! You ghosts sure know how to live it up.

LORD TERENCE. Owww! A ghost can't live it up. Owww—

LADY GRANIA. Oww! A ghost can't live it up. Owww—

OTHER GHOSTS. Oww. A ghost can't live it up. Oww— (*All weep. They form line and march out, saying,* "Oww, a ghost can't live it up. Owww!" Mike *and* Molly *follow them to the exit saying,* "Come back. 'Live it up' is just an expression. Come back." Mike *and* Molly *return to sofa as last ghost disappears. They sit limp and sad, not saying or noticing anything, just looking straight ahead.* Mr. Terwinkle *enters, carrying long chains.*)

MR. TERWINKLE. Look what I found in the basement—I mean, dungeon. Chains.

(Mrs. Terwinkle *enters with skeleton, either a plastic one or black cloth or paper with a skeleton painted on it.*)

MRS. TERWINKLE. Look what I found in the closet. A skeleton! Such housekeepers. (Mike *and* Molly *pay no attention to parents.*)

MR. TERWINKLE. What's the matter with you two?

MRS. TERWINKLE. You look as if you had seen a ghost.

MOLLY AND MIKE. We did! We saw several ghosts!

MIKE. Real ghosts!

MOLLY. Lord Terence and Lady Grania O'Toole and their friends.

MRS. TERWINKLE. Where?

MOLLY. Right here.

MIKE. All over.

MR. TERWINKLE. When?

MOLLY. While you were out.

MRS. TERWINKLE. And what did you do with ghosts?

MIKE. We danced the Irish jig.

MR. AND MRS. TERWINKLE. The Irish jig?

MOLLY. Yes, the ghosts taught us to dance the Irish jig.

MIKE. And then I said, "You ghosts sure know how to live it up."

MOLLY. And the ghosts cried and said, "A ghost can't live it up."

MIKE. Then the ghosts went away.

MOLLY. They wouldn't stay.

MR. TERWINKLE (*looking at his wife*). You know, Maude, it's true. "Once a Texan, always a Texan."

MRS. TERWINKLE. You're right. When it comes to telling tall tales, you're right. Ghosts, indeed!

MR. TERWINKLE. Dancing the Irish jig! They can't live it up, and with that story we won't be able to live it down.

(*Curtain is pulled as* Mike *and* Molly *are saying,* "Honest, Mom. Honest, Dad. We did dance the Irish jig." *They start to dance as parents are showing disgust at the idea of ghosts.*)

GOODBYE, SNIKKE-SNAK

Introduction

The actors in this play have an opportunity to express a variety of emotions: joy of living, fear, anxiety, concern for the feeling of another person, determination, and, finally, triumph. They must express these emotions with their body movements, tone of voice, and facial expressions. In order to do this each actor must try to put himself into the place of another person and try to feel as he probably would feel.

Before learning lines, practice picking flowers and moving about the stage in a happy mood. Strangely enough, this is often the hardest mood to portray. The opening scene must move quickly.

Music may help you capture this opening mood. Play a record that makes you think of spring. Move in time to the music. Now practice picking imaginary flowers. Remember, the stems are tiny. You must not crush the flowers. Once you feel at home on the stage, practice your lines.

Study the different qualities of the two girls. Nina, the older, should be taller, and she should act older, too. How does she do this? Kirstin is younger, but not babyish. Show by the tone of her voice that she looks up to and admires Nina.

Granny must seem older than the girls in her actions as well as her appearance. She is not a feeble old lady. How are you to make her appear mature?

Snikke-Snak is mean from start to finish, but she does have a strain of fairness in her. She likes to bargain and she stops now and then to figure out what proposition she will offer.

In appearance, she is a European witch, not a Halloween witch. If the play is produced in costume, she will wear a dark, hooded cape, a long dark skirt, and a dark apron with a pocket large enough to hold her knitting. She can use her cape effectively to accent her emotions. For example, she can fling it out wide when she thinks she has tricked the girls. She can pull it around her tightly when she is defeated.

The trolls are stooped, ugly, underworld creatures with no strain of happiness or fairness in them. They frown constantly. If the trolls are to add atmosphere to the play, each must remain ugly every minute. The audience may laugh when they first appear, but the trolls must remain in their ugly positions until all is quiet. The trolls may be able to perfect their marching by stamping in time to somber music.

If a group wishes to produce the play without the trolls, omit all the conversation with the trolls and open the second scene with Snikke-Snak sitting on the stump knitting and mumbling to herself: "Click, clack! Snikke-snak! I'm going to take the maiden back."

If you wish, two boys or a boy and a girl could play the parts of Nina and Kirstin by a simple change of names.

Characters

NINA, Danish girl, nine to twelve years old
KIRSTIN, her little sister
GRANNY, their grandmother
SNIKKE-SNAK, Witch of Field and Forest
TROLLS

SCENE I. *A field at the edge of a forest in Denmark, years ago. The time is early spring. Right, downstage, is a large rock or tree stump on which characters can sit. If it is made of paper-mache, it must have a box or some other solid foundation. Other smaller rocks with bits of green around them are placed here and there.*

Flowers are placed behind the rocks. As the scene opens, Nina *and* Kirstin *enter happily and look around in wonder.*

NINA. Oh, Kirstin, isn't it beautiful?

KIRSTIN. I've never been here before.

NINA. I know. This is the field. (*Points to background.*) There is the forest.

KIRSTIN. It's different from Granny's garden.

NINA. Oh, yes, very different. Let's look for wild flowers.

KIRSTIN. Wild flowers? I don't see any wild flowers.

NINA. Of course not. The first wild flowers are very tiny. You have to look for them. (*Runs to small rock and bends down.*) Look, Kirstin, I found some. Come and pick them.

KIRSTIN (*running to rock and picking a few flowers*). Oh, aren't they pretty! (Nina *runs to another rock.*)

NINA. Look, more! (Kirstin *happily picks those flowers as* Nina *looks behind the large stump or stone downstage.*) And some more! (Kirstin *comes to pick these flowers as* Nina *sits on stump or stone and looks around.*) Oh, Kirstin, did you ever see any place more beautiful?

KIRSTIN. It is pretty, but it's a long way from Granny's cottage. Granny warned us never to leave the cottage. (*Sits at* Nina's *feet and looks at her flowers.*)

NINA. I'm sorry, Kirstin. I know it's wrong, but I had to come. I had to see the open field and the forest again.

KIRSTIN. Why, Nina?

NINA. I'll tell you. Long ago, before you were born, Father, Mother, and I lived near this field. Every spring we came here to look for the first wild flowers. Mother always found them, but she let me pick them. Father stood guard, looking into the forest.

KIRSTIN. Why did Father stand guard?

NINA (*wondering*). I really don't know. (*Quickens speech.*) Then came the summer you were born. We were all very happy. Then Mother died and Father died, and you and I went to live with Granny.

KIRSTIN. And Granny always said, "Don't go near the forest because an old witch lives there."

NINA. That's a granny tale.

KIRSTIN. A what?

NINA. A granny tale. A story that grandmothers tell the children to make them stay near home. She says there's a horrible witch in the forest. Folks call her Snikke-Snak.

KIRSTIN. Why Snikke-Snak?

NINA. Because when she talks she always says "snikke-snak," like we say "fiddlesticks."

KIRSTIN. What's wrong with that?

NINA. Nothing, maybe. But folks say the witch rules a band of trolls, who live underground all winter long. When the first flowers bloom in the field or forest, the witch and the trolls come up to the top of the earth.

KIRSTIN. I should think so.

NINA. Now, listen to the end of the granny tale. If the witch finds a mortal picking the first spring flowers, she commands the trolls to drag the mortal underground. The mortal has to work for the witch and the trolls all winter long.

KIRSTIN. Oh, how dreadful, that Snikke-Snak!

NINA. Yes, dreadful. However, she has one good point. If she makes a bargain she keeps it. So if you ever meet Snikke-Snak, try to bargain with her. (Snikke-Snak *enters from upstage and creeps behind the girls, unseen by them.*)

KIRSTIN (*rising*). Snikke-Snak! Snikke-Snak! Who believes in Snikke-Snak?

SNIKKE-SNAK (*pointing finger at* Kirstin). YOU! (Snikke-Snak *stalks around left stage, turns suddenly, points finger at* Kirstin.) Don't you call me Snikke-Snak. (Nina *steps forward bravely, guarding her younger sister who stands behind her, cringing with fear.* Snikke-Snak *comes slowly toward the girls, pointing to* Kirstin.) You, you little one. You have been picking my wild flowers.

NINA. Please. Please, she didn't know they were your flowers.

SNIKKE-SNAK. Snikke-snak! Snikke-snak! All mortals know that I own the first wild flowers in the field and forest.

NINA. Please. Please, she's never been in the field and forest before. She had never seen the first wild flowers until today.

SNIKKE-SNAK. Snikke-snak! Snikke-snak! Don't talk to me! I never pay attention to what children say—or old folks either. I want the girl who picked my flowers.

NINA. Oh, no! No! Don't take her! She's too little. Take me. I showed her where to find the flowers.

SNIKKE-SNAK. Snikke-snak. What a lot of talk. (*She turns. Paces the floor as if thinking, and then comes back to the girls.*) You are right. She is too little to work hard. I'll take you.

KIRSTIN. No! (*Nina stands firm.*)

SNIKKE-SNAK. I'll have you work beneath the ground and serve the trolls and me.

NINA. Oh, thank you, Snikke-Snak.

SNIKKE-SNAK. Don't you call me Snikke-Snak!

NINA. Well, Witch of the Field and Forest, I must agree that you are very wise to choose me. (Snikke-Snak *shakes her head proudly.*) But don't you think it is foolish to take me now?

SNIKKE-SNAK. Why?

NINA (*slowly as if thinking of a reason*). Because— it's much too lovely out-of-doors right now. Don't witches and trolls want to be out-of-doors on a day like this, when wild flowers are blooming? Which of you would stay underground to guard me?

SNIKKE-SNAK. You are right. You would be useless now. (*Paces floor.*) All right, I'll make a bargain. You may stay above the ground as long as flowers are blooming.

NINA. Any flower? Any place?

SNIKKE-SNAK. Any flower, out-of-doors in Denmark. But when the last flower fades in the out-of-doors, I'll come and get you.

NINA. Please, good witch, don't come and get me. Let me meet you here.

SNIKKE-SNAK. Why?

NINA. I don't want Granny to see you. I don't want Granny to worry when she finds that I am gone. Let her think that I just left home.

SNIKKE-SNAK. All right. I'll meet you here, when the last flower fades in the out-of-doors. However, if you do not come, I'll come to your cottage, with all the trolls, and get you. (*Points to first* Nina, *then* Kirstin.) And you! And your Granny, too. (*She stalks upstage, turns, and yells.*) I'll see you when the last flower fades in the out-of-doors. (*Exits. Sisters stand as if paralyzed until* Kirstin *starts to cry.*)

KIRSTIN. Nina, Nina, what will you do?

NINA (*bravely*). I don't know. (*Straightens her shoulders as if gathering strength to comfort her little sister.*) Enjoy the spring flowers, Kirstin, and the summer and the autumn flowers in Granny's garden.

KIRSTIN. And when winter comes?

NINA. Who knows? Remember, we must not let Granny worry. (*Girls exit sadly as curtain falls.*)

SCENE II. *The same field in the dead of winter. Leaves are scattered on the ground. One pile is downstage center. As the scene opens,* Snikke-Snak *sits on the large stump, knitting a long black scarf. The ball of yarn is in her big apron pocket.* Trolls *enter from the back in a long line, stamp, and chant in unison, as if in time to the witch's knitting.*

TROLLS. Click, clack!
Snikke-snak!
We're going to take
The maiden back.
Click, clack!
Snikke-snak!
We're going to take,
The maiden back!

(*They continue chanting until they have formed a line across the stage.* Trolls *with speaking parts step forward.*)

TROLL 1. Well, where is she?

SNIKKE-SNAK. She'll come. She'll come.

TROLL 2 (*mocking witch*). "She'll come! She'll come!" Every day you say, "She'll come." You and your bargains!

TROLL 3. Did you ever get a mortal to work for us?

OTHER TROLLS. No!

TROLL 4. All winter we toil beneath the ground.

TROLL 5. You catch a mortal, then you make a bargain. She beats you at the bargain. You let her go free. (*Other trolls grumble.*)

SNIKKE-SNAK. Snikke-snak, snikke-snak! This time she won't go free. Who can find a flower blooming out-of-doors in weather like this? Ha-Ha-Ha! Shhh—(*Motions* Trolls *to step back*). Here she comes—and her sister—and would you look? Her Granny, too. I'll make a bargain and get them all. (Trolls *stand glowering upstage as girls and* Granny *enter sadly.*)

SNIKKE-SNAK. So—you were long in coming.

NINA (*nodding*). Yes, Snikke-Snak.

SNIKKE-SNAK. Don't you call me Snikke-Snak.

NINA. Witch of the Field and Forest, I'd like you to meet my Granny. (Granny *nods.*) You know Kirstin.

SNIKKE-SNAK. So you told your granny. Do you think she'll worry?

NINA. She always worries when we're gone. I told her today.

GRANNY (*with arm around* Nina). Of course, I had to come.

KIRSTIN. And so did I.

SNIKKE-SNAK. Well, what took you so long?

NINA (*brightly*). First there were the flowers of spring, and they were beautiful.

SNIKKE-SNAK. Beautiful? Useful to catch a mortal.

NINA. Then came summer, and Granny's garden was full of flowers. One rose bloomed and bloomed and bloomed, long after all the other garden flowers had faded.

SNIKKE-SNAK. There's always one silly rose that blooms and blooms and blooms.

NINA. The asters along the road blossomed late this year, and after that, the weather turned surprisingly warm. The foolish witch hazel thought it was spring and burst into bloom.

SNIKKE-SNAK. It did, indeed. However, now it is winter, dead freezing winter. Every flower in the out-of-doors is faded. You must come with me.

GRANNY. Wait. Wait, let us look once more. Let us all look.

SNIKKE-SNAK. Look for a flower? Where?

GRANNY. Beneath the snow, beneath the leaves and sticks.

SNIKKE-SNAK. Snikke-snak! (*She has second thought.*) Wait, old woman. I'll make a bargain. If you can find one flower blooming in this winter wild, I'll let you all go free.

GRANNY. Free forever?

SNIKKE-SNAK. Well, yes. If you can find one blooming flower, I'll never leave the underworld again.

TROLLS (*with disgust*). Ughhhhhh—

SNIKKE-SNAK. However, if you do not find one flower, I'll take you all to toil beneath the ground.

TROLLS. Yeah!

(Granny *and the girls fall quickly to their knees, paying no*

attention to Trolls *or* Witch *as they frantically push leaves aside.*)

GRANNY. Nina! Kirstin! Look! (Nina *kneels beside her and slowly lifts a flower. All stand in wonder.* Snikke-Snak *comes close to look, not believing what she sees.*

GRANNY. It's a Christmas rose.

SNIKKE-SNAK. A Christmas rose? I never heard of a Christmas rose or any other flower blooming in mid-winter.

GRANNY. Of course, you haven't, or you wouldn't have made your bargain.

SNIKKE-SNAK. Bargain?

KIRSTIN. Yes, bargain, Witch of the Field and Forest.

NINA. You promised to stay underground forever if we found one flower blooming. Luckily, we found a Christmas rose!

GRANNY. Now how about your bargain? To go underground forever.

TROLLS (*in ugly manner*). Yes, what a bargain! To go underground forever. (Witch *becomes frantic. Raises her hands as she screams.*)

SNIKKE-SNAK. BAR-gain! Eeeeeeeeeeeee! Underground forever! Eeeeeeeeeeee! (*She paces back and forth, waving her hands in the air and repeating these phrases until* Troll 1 *steps in front of her and shakes his finger at her.*)

TROLL 1. I warned you, Snikke-Snak. You and your bargains. You've put us underground forever!

SNIKKE-SNAK. Underground forever! Eeeeeee! (*She exits, her screams getting fainter as* Troll 1 *speaks to other trolls.*)

TROLL 1. Like it or not, we have to follow Snikke-Snak. Underground forever. (Trolls *form a snake-chain and weave back and forth across the stage gradually reaching the exit as they chant.*)

TROLLS. Snikke-Snak, Snikke-Snak,
Underground forever!
Snikke-Snak, won't be back.
Never! Never! Never!

(They continue to chant until all of the trolls are offstage.)

(Granny *and girls stand close together and at an angle so that each may be seen.* Kirstin *is farthest downstage and* Nina *is in the center, still holding the Christmas rose tenderly in both hands. As the last troll makes his exit,* Kirstin *raises her hand slightly and calls.*)

Kirstin. Goodbye, Snikke-Snak, Witch of the Field and Forest.

Nina. Goodbye forever.

Granny. And ever!

(All three glance at rose admiringly as curtain closes.)

—*Goodbye, Snikke Snak* is based on an old Danish tale.

WHY THE LEAVES OF THE ASPEN TREE QUAKE IN A BREEZE

Introduction

Each group of American Indians has its own legends. The tales of various tribes are similar in certain ways. Frequently the storyteller explains why something happens in nature. Often a human being is punished or rewarded by being turned into a bird, animal, tree, or star. In this Algonquin Indian legend, a selfish sister is turned into a quaking aspen tree.

As in many folktales, there is a conflict between two sisters—one proud and selfish, the other kind and thoughtful. The audience must at once sense the difference between the sisters. The action and the spoken lines will make the difference clear.

PLAY A PART

Misticoosis, the selfish sister, should practice walking in a proud manner and snapping out her lines. Omemee, the patient sister, must express gentleness in the tone of her voice, as well as in her actions. Her eyes must shine when she is happy. She must show from first to last that she is a loving person.

Misticoosis' continued shaking at the close of the play may cause problems. She must make her fright and her trembling seem real. The other members of the cast must also consider her shaking real. However, they don't feel sorry for her. The Indians no doubt think that she deserves her punishment.

If the audience laughs at Misticoosis' shaking, ignore the laughter. Adlib lines and show confusion (not amusement) until the audience is quiet enough for actors to make themselves heard.

Make the scene as realistic as you please. Moccasins must be decorated. A basic design can be taped onto the top of a moccasin. In adding pieces, Omemee can use small plastic strips, softening them between her teeth as the Indians softened porcupine quills. Or she can use small strips of colored paper. Necklaces worn by Algonquin women were made of shells, claws, bones, or leather strips decorated with quillwork.

If you wish to learn more about Algonquin costumes, consult a reference book, such as *Indians* by Edwin Tunis, World Publishing Company.

Characters

MISTICOOSIS, a proud and selfish Algonquin Indian maiden
OMEMEE, her thoughtful sister
FATHER, an Algonquin chief
WAKONDAS, son of a Great Spirit
STORYTELLER

SCENE. *Inside a wigwam. A fur rug is placed center front. To the back, and to one side, are two wooden or stone bowls. One holds a small leather pouch and the other some dried corn. The* Storyteller *steps in front of the drawn curtain.*

STORYTELLER. Do you know why the leaves of an aspen tree quake in a breeze? Listen and you shall learn.

(*As the scene opens,* Omemee *is seen sitting a little left of center front. She sings softly as she adds porcupine quills to a design on a moccasin. She pauses, picks up both moccasins, and holds them at arms' length admiringly.*

Misticoosis *enters right, strutting, smoothing her hair, and fingering her beads. She looks down haughtily at her sister, who has not noticed her entrance.*)

MISTICOOSIS. They're nice. Sturdy. Neat.

OMEMEE. Thank you. They are a most beautiful pair of moccasins, if I do say so myself. (*Sets moccasins on floor.*) Where have you been?

MISTICOOSIS. To the pond.

OMEMEE. The pond! Why the pond? There's work to do at the wigwam.

MISTICOOSIS. And you, little Sit-by-the-Fire, are the one to do the work. (*Struts a little.*) But why did I go to the pond?

OMEMEE. Yes, why? There's nothing to gather this time of year.

MISTICOOSIS. Nothing to gather! (*Walks as she talks.*) Work, always work. You think of nothing but work. (*Turns toward her sister.*) If you must know, I went to the pond to see my reflection. I am a most beautiful maiden.

OMEMEE. Beauty is as beauty does.

MISTICOOSIS. How little you know, Omemee. Well, you may land a husband yet. Someone may like your moccasins. A widowed warrior. An untested brave. But I, Misticoosis, intend to marry Wakondas.

OMEMEE (*shocked*). Wakondas! (*Stands.*) Sister, Wakondas is the son of Wakonda, the most powerful spirit. How can you hope to marry Wakondas?

MISTICOOSIS. I not only hope. I plan to marry Wakondas because I am the most beautiful Indian princess in the north country.

OMEMEE (*slowly*). I, too, am a princess.

MISTICOOSIS. Yes, you are a cook-by-the-fire princess. Your face is brown with smoke. You are a work-all-the-time princess. Your fingers are rough from pulling thongs to make moccasins. (Omemee *lowers her head and looks sadly at moccasins of which she had been so proud.* Misticoosis *is suddenly sorry for what she has said and puts her arm around her sister.*) There, don't feel bad . . . (*Picks up a moccasin.*) Your quill work is lovely. (*Drops moccasin and fingers one necklace.*) Wakondas will admire the quill necklace you made for me.

OMEMEE. How will you meet Wakondas?

MISTICOOSIS. Wakondas is a spirit as well as a man. Wakondas will find me.

WAKONDAS (*in the voice of old man*). Misticoosis! Omemee!

OMEMEE. Who can it be?

MISTICOOSIS. Sounds like some old man.

WAKONDAS (*offstage*). Misticoosis! Omemee! I am tired of traveling. May I come in? (*Sisters speak together.*)

MISTICOOSIS. Depends. Who are you?

OMEMEE. Of course you may come in!

(Wakondas *enters disguised as an old man.*)

MISTICOOSIS (*in disgust*). Who on earth are you?

WAKONDAS. I am a weary traveler from the land of the West.

OMEMEE. You poor old man. Sit on this rug. (*She helps him to sit.*)

MISTICOOSIS. I say, "Go back to the land of the West." You are ready to die. Go back to the West!

OMEMEE. You are faint. (*Gets pouch. Hands him a morsel.*) Chew this slowly.

WAKONDAS. Thank you.

MISTICOOSIS. You are giving him dried venison!

OMEMEE. Yes, he needs food.

MISTICOOSIS. He needs food? We need food! That dried venison and that corn (*pointing to bowl*) are all the food we have in the wigwam. Old man, get out of here. Get out! Get out of this wigwam!

OMEMEE. He can't go, sister. Look at his feet. He's wearing rags, not moccasins. (*She unwinds rags and picks up new moccasins.*)

MISTICOOSIS. Sister! You made those moccasins for a bridegroom. I know you made them for a bridegroom.

OMEMEE. Who cares? This old man needs moccasins more than I need a bridegroom. (*Puts moccasins on old man.*) There, old man.

WAKONDAS. Thank you. Thank you. (*Rises.*) I can go now. May the spirits bless you, Omemee. (*Stands up straight and speaks in a loud clear voice.*) And may the spirits curse you, Misticoosis! (*Exits.* Misticoosis *is angry.* Omemee *seems dazed.*)

MISTICOOSIS. He put a curse on me. Now how do you like that? A foolish old man put a curse on me.

OMEMEE (*as in a trance*). Was he foolish? Was he old?

MISTICOOSIS. Who cares? You gave away moccasins! You gave away food. You think an old man is more important than your family! (Omemee *goes backstage to get bowl of corn as her sister follows her around. They come downstage center.*) What will we eat?

OMEMEE. There's a little corn. I'll prepare it.

(Misticoosis *continues to scold until she is interrupted by offstage voice.*)

MISTICOOSIS. Don't spill that corn! Be careful of that corn! That corn is precious—

FATHER (*offstage*). Misticoosis! Omemee!

MISTICOOSIS AND OMEMEE. It's Father.

MISTICOOSIS. Wait until he hears what you did!

OMEMEE. He'll be glad. (Omemee *sets bowl backstage as* Misticoosis *smooths her hair and clothing. Their father, the chief, enters with* Wakondas, *now dressed as a young brave and wearing moccasins* Omemee *has given him.*)

FATHER. May I introduce my daughters. Omemee. (*She smiles and nods.*) Misticoosis. (*She smiles and nods.*) Daughters, may I present Wakondas.

OMEMEE AND MISTICOOSIS (*together*). Wakondas!

FATHER. Daughters, bow your heads in the presence of a brave who is both man and spirit. (*Girls lower their eyes and both notice* Wakondas' *moccasins.* Father *continues to talk until he realizes that something is happening.*) Wakondas, I must apologize. My daughters—

(OMEMEE *gasps softly.*)

OMEMEE. My moccasins! (*She slowly raises her head until her eyes meet those of* Wakondas *who is smiling at her. At the same time* Misticoosis *notices the moccasins and begins to yell and shake.*)

MISTICOOSIS. The moccasins! Her moccasins! The old man's moccasins. No! No! No! (*She continues to shake and say,* "No! No! No!" *more softly as others talk.*)

FATHER. Omemee, Misticoosis, what is the meaning of this? What is wrong with his moccasins?

WAKONDAS. Nothing is wrong with my moccasins. They are beautiful.

FATHER. Then what is wrong with Misticoosis?

WAKONDAS. Let me explain. I came to your wigwam disguised as a weary old man. Misticoosis promptly yelled, "Get out!" Omemee begged me to rest on a rug. Omemee fed me. And Omemee gave me these moccasins. I am in love with Omemee, and I want to marry her.

FATHER. I understand. Omemee, do you wish to marry Wakodas?

OMEMEE. Oh yes, Father.

FATHER. Then marry with my blessing. Let us tell the tribe. (Father, Omemee, *and* Wakondas *exit. All this time* Misticoosis *has been shaking and murmuring* "No!" *Now she yells.*)

MISTICOOSIS. What about me? What about me?

(Wakondas *reenters. With a dramatic gesture, he extends his backstage arm and points his finger at* Misticoosis.)

WAKONDAS. You, Misticoosis, vain and selfish maiden. You shall become a quaking aspen tree. In the winter your limbs will be bare. In the summer your leaves shall quake in the breeze. Cursed be the Indian maiden who is vain and selfish.

(WAKONDAS *exits as* Misticoosis *continues to shake. The curtain is drawn as the* Storyteller *steps to the front of the stage.*)

STORYTELLER. To this day the leaves of the aspen tree quake each time a small wind blows.

—*Why the Leaves of the Aspen Tree Quake in a Breeze* is based on an Algonquin Indian legend.

PLAY A PART

TO SMILE FROM HER HEART

Introduction

The story of a princess who will not smile is an old, old tale found in different versions in different lands. In this play the princess refuses to laugh at the tricks or funny situations provided by the people who want her to smile. Eventually she learns to smile from her heart.

Hopefully, the audience will be amused by the scowling, stamping princess and will laugh at the people who try to discover why she does not smile. The situation will be funny only if every member of the cast considers an unpleasant princess a serious national problem.

The role of Princess Alicia presents a challenge because this self-centered, spoiled young lady must change gradually into a person interested in the welfare of others. She must become as radiantly happy at the end of the play as she was stubbornly angry at the beginning.

Honora is a delicate role of both servant and friend. She must speak out, but she must also remember her lowly place in the palace.

The king is very much like his daughter. He is a man who knows what he wants and is in the habit of commanding others to do his will. However, he is capable of growth. He recognizes a problem when he sees one, and he is grateful to anyone who can help him.

The Queen Mother and Honora's mother are the best of mothers, concerned about others and willing to do anything to help. The Prince and cousin Nathanial are charming as princes should be.

The characters of Hairdresser, Seamstress, Cosmetologist, Jester, and Wizard must be exaggerated. They are on center stage for only brief periods. However, they must remain constantly in character as they fade into the background group.

There may be only one or two knights and ladies or as many more as you wish. Additional porters could be added to help the Prince and his cousin carry clothing back to Stillhope in the kingdom of Mountavalia.

Characters

PRINCESS ALICIA
THE QUEEN, her mother
THE KING, her father
HONORA, her Maid-in-Waiting
MOTHER OF HONORA
OTHER WOMEN OF KINGDOM
LADIES OF COURT AND KNIGHTS
HAIRDRESSER
SEAMSTRESS
COSMETOLOGIST
JESTER
WIZARD
PRINCE CHRISTOFFO
NATHANIAL, his cousin
PAGE

SCENE. *Garden of the palace. A garden bench, large enough to seat two people, is placed downstage center. As the scene opens,* Princess Alicia *is screaming and pacing back and forth across the stage. The* Queen, Alicia's *mother, and* Honora *try to subdue her. Maidens and knights shake their heads with great concern.*

PRINCESS ALICIA. It's terrible. Disgraceful. I'm outraged! Disgusted! Flabbergasted! (*Pauses midstage.*) I'm just plain mad!

HONORA. Please, please, mistress!

PRINCESS ALICIA (*mockingly*). Please, please. Who tries to please me? Nobody! Nobody! Nobody! I won't stand for it!

QUEEN. Daughter, daughter, I entreat you. Be reasonable.

PRINCESS ALICIA. Reasonable? Why should I be reasonable? Why? Why? Why?

(King *enters left. Stops before he reaches center stage.*)

KING (*with force*). Wait a minute! Quiet! (Princess Alicia *stops yelling and looks at her father angrily. Others bow slightly from waist.*) What goes on here? (Queen *steps forward, bows, and rises.*)

QUEEN. Sire, your daughter is angry.

KING. So I perceive. What is the trouble?

PRINCESS ALICIA. It is Wednesday.

KING. Yes, every seventh day is Wednesday.

PRINCESS ALICIA. And in three days it will be Saturday. (King *shows no reaction.*) Saturday, the twenty-first.

KING. Yes, in three days it will be Saturday, the twenty-first.

PRINCESS ALICIA. Saturday, the twenty-first, is the day of the ball.

KING. True. Every year this kingdom holds a ball. Now what is the problem? (*Silence.*)

KING (*shouting*). What is the problem? (*Silence.*) You, madam— (Queen *steps forward and faces him.*) You are her mother. Tell me. What is the problem?

QUEEN. This year the ball is dedicated to beautiful maidens.

KING. Yes, this year the ball is dedicated to beautiful maidens.

QUEEN. Our daughter has not been invited.

KING. Not invited? Why? (*Silence.*) Why?

PRINCESS ALICIA (*frowning*). Say it, Mother. (*Steps forward.*) If you won't, I will. I have not been invited to attend the Ball of the Beautiful Maidens because I am not beautiful.

KING. Oh, let me consider this. Come here. (Alicia *comes center stage as the* Queen *steps back.* King *stands with his feet apart, hands on his hips, looking at* Princess Alicia, *who continues to frown.*) Mmmmmmmm— (King *walks around her, looking at her.*) Mmmmmmm— (*He stands looking at her again.*) Mmmmmmm—Not beautiful—(Alicia *glares at him.*) Perhaps you are right. (Princess Alicia *stamps her foot.*) Surely something can be done about this situation—and before Saturday night. Sit down, daughter. Sit down. (Alicia *sits on bench.*) I command someone to make my daughter beautiful. (*Silence.*) Well, do something! Do something! (Queen *steps forward.*)

QUEEN. Perhaps the hairdresser could do something. (King *claps hands.*)

KING (*impatiently*). Hairdresser! Hairdresser! (Hairdresser *enters right, quickly. Bows before* King.)

KING. Hairdresser, rise. We have observed that our daughter is not beautiful. What can you do?

HAIRDRESSER. I'll see, Your Majesty. (*He walks with little steps around the* Princess *who continues to frown. Pats her hair. Returns to* King.) I am sorry, sire. Her hair is perfect. (*Turns and looks at* Princess *who makes a face.*) But I must admit. She is not beautiful. (*All maidens and knights shake their heads and sigh, as* Hairdresser *joins them and* Queen *speaks.*)

QUEEN. It might be her clothing.

KING (*clapping hands*). Dressmaker! Dressmaker! (Dressmaker *enters quickly from right. Bows.*) Dressmaker, rise. We have observed that our daughter is not beautiful. What can you do to make her beautiful?

DRESSMAKER. I'll see, sire. (*Walks with little steps to* Princess.) Please arise, Your Majesty. (Princess Alicia *stands.* Dressmaker *walks around her quickly, touching gown here and there. Returns to* King.) I'm sorry, sire. The clothing of the Princess Alicia appears to be perfect. (*Turns and looks again at* Princess *who glares at her.*) But I must admit. She is not beautiful. (*Maidens and knights shake heads as* Dressmaker *joins them and* Queen *speaks.*)

QUEEN. Do you think, sire, it could be her face?

KING. Maybe! Maybe. (*Claps hands.*) Cosmetologist! Cosmetologist! (Cosmetologist *enters with ruler or caliper. Bows before* King.) Cosmetologist, rise. We have observed that our daughter is not beautiful. Can you discover the reason?

COSMETOLOGIST. I can try, sire. (*Goes to* Princess *who is still seated and frowning. Measures the length and breadth of her face.*) Perfect! The proportions of her face are perfect. (*Measures her nose.*) Perfect! Her nose is perfect. (*Measures her mouth.*) Perfect! Perfect! (*Pinches her cheek gently.*) Perfect. Sire, everything about your daughter's face is perfect. (*Looks at her again as she scowls.*) Yet I must admit she is not beautiful. I cannot help her. (*Joins others backstage.*)

KING. Call the Wizard. Wizard! Wizard! (Wizard *enters. Bows low.*) Wizard, we have a problem. Our daughter is not beautiful. You must make her beautiful.

WIZARD. I shall try, sire. (*Goes to* Princess *who scowls at him. Returns slowly to King.*) Sire—

KING. Speak!

WIZARD. Your daughter is not beautiful because she does not smile.

KING. Oh, well! Thank you, Wizard. Thank you. (*Claps hands.*) Jester! Jester! (Jester *enters quickly.*) Jester, do some tricks. Make my daughter smile. (Jester *does some handsprings, jumps up and down. Court people and workers laugh.* Princess Alicia *shows disgust.* Wizard *shakes his head.*)

KING (*to* Jester). Stop! (*To* Wizard) Why are you shaking your head?

WIZARD. You do not understand, sire. In order to be beautiful, the Princess Alicia must smile from her heart.

KING (*thoughtfully to* Queen). Smile from her heart. (*To* Wizard) Now what can we do about that?

WIZARD. Nothing, sire. Nothing. Only the Princess can discover how to smile from her heart. Please excuse me. (*Bows. Exits right.*)

KING. Nothing? Nothing? Never let it be said that I the King can do nothing. I know. I shall offer a reward. Hear, ye! I now proclaim—the person who can make the Princess Alicia smile from her heart shall become a Prince or Princess of the Grand Order.

(PRINCESS ALICIA *glowers. Honora is bewildered. All others are excited and seem to mouth.* "The Grand Order, Oh!" "What can we do?")

QUEEN. Sire, you are wonderful! Surely someone will think of something.

KING. Let us hope so, Your Highness. Shall we leave? (*He offers her his arm. She places her arm on his. They exit majestically followed by court and workers.* Princess Alicia *and* Honora *remain.* Alicia, *sitting on bench, starts to cry. She sobs wildly. Soon* Honora, *standing beside her is crying too.* Alicia *stops suddenly.*)

PRINCESS ALICIA. And why, may I ask, are *you* crying? (Honora *tries to stifle her sobs.*) Are you crying because I can't go to the ball? (Honora, *still sniffling, shakes her head.*) You're not? Are you crying because you can't go to the ball? (Honora *shakes her head.*) Then, why are you crying? (Honora *chokes.*) Here, sit down. (Honora *sits next to the* Princess.) That's better. Now tell me, why are you crying?

HONORA. I'm thinking about my mother's people.

PRINCESS ALICIA. Your mother's people? Where do they live?

HONORA. In the village of Stillhope in the Kingdom of Mountavalia.

PRINCESS ALICIA. Mountavalia is a very good land, almost as good as ours.

HONORA. I know. And Stillhope was a very good village until— (*She begins to cry again.*)

PRINCESS. Until what? Stop crying and tell me what happened.

HONORA (*choking sobs*). My mother just heard. A week ago all the people were attending services in the chapel on the mountaintop. Suddenly, down below, there was a landslide. It started slowly, then went faster and faster, down the mountainside, crashing, rolling, destroying everything that lay in its path.

PRINCESS ALICIA. Everything?

HONORA. Everything. Houses, barns, livestock, food stored for the coming winter. All that the people have left is the clothes on their backs.

PRINCESS ALICIA. How dreadful! Well, Mountavalia has a king. Can't the king do something?

HONORA. Oh, indeed. The king, his sons, and all the other men in Mountavalia are building new homes for the people of Stillhope.

PRINCESS ALICIA. And the women? Can't they do something?

HONORA. Oh, yes. The women are busy from dawn to dark tending gardens and livestock, producing food for everyone in Mountavalia.

PRINCESS ALICIA. That's wonderful! Now the people of Stillhope have no problems.

HONORA. Oh, Your Majesty, you are mistaken.

PRINCESS ALICIA. Mistaken? The people will soon have food and shelter.

HONORA. But they have no clothes, except the clothes on their backs.

PRINCESS ALICIA. Clothes? (*She smiles for first time.*) That's easy. I have chests and chests of clothes. They shall have mine.

HONORA. You mean it? Really?

PRINCESS. Yes, really!

HONORA. Wonderful! Except—

PRINCESS ALICIA. Except what?

HONORA. To speak truly, Your Majesty, your clothes aren't suitable for the people of Stillhope.

PRINCESS ALICIA (*rising angrily*). You mean that my clothes aren't good enough for the people of Stillhope?

HONORA (*rising, too*). Oh, no, no. I said your clothes aren't suitable. The people of Stillhope are mountain people. They need sturdy, warm clothes, linens and wools. Your clothes are made of silks, brocades, velvets— (Princess Alicia *plumps down on the bench.*)

PRINCESS ALICIA. There ought to be something we could use. Silks indeed! (*Brushes her dress. Lifts skirt a little. Looks at petticoat.*) Look, Honora, isn't this linen? It's sturdy.

HONORA (*feeling petticoat*). It is, indeed.

PRINCESS ALICIA (*standing*). I know. I'll order every seamstress to make clothing for the people of Stillhope. They can use petticoats, sheets, woolen blankets, new material—anything sturdy that they can find. Every seamstress—

HONORA. Wonderful! (*Pauses.*) Except—

PRINCESS ALICIA. Except what?

HONORA. Every seamstress is busy making dresses for the ball.

PRINCESS ALICIA (*stamping her foot*). That ball! Don't make me angry again. What can we do?

HONORA. My mother is making over everything she can.

PRINCESS ALICIA. That's it! Your mother shall come here and make clothing for the people of Stillhope, and I shall embroider the baby dresses.

HONORA. Your Majesty, may I make a suggestion?

PRINCESS ALICIA (*enthusiastically*). Of course! Of course!

HONORA. If you can embroider you can sew a straight seam. That's what the people of Stillhope need now. Plain garments with straight seams.

PRINCESS ALICIA. Of course. And if I sew garments with straight seams, other maidens and women will sew garments with straight seams. Honora, in three days' time we should have sturdy clothing for the people of Stillhope.

HONORA. Yes, yes.

PRINCESS ALICIA (*calling*). Jester! (Jester *appears, right.*) Jester, you can jump and you can tumble. Can you run?

JESTER. Yes, Your Highness, I can run like the wind.

PRINCESS ALICIA. Then I command you. Run like the wind to the kingdom of Mountavalia! Tell His Majesty, the King, that in three days' time we shall have clothing for the people of Stillhope. Run! Run!

JESTER. Yes, Your Majesty. (*Exits running.*)

PRINCESS ALICIA. Honora, Honora! (*She grasps her hands at arm's length.*) We shall soon have clothing for the people of Stillhope. Isn't that wonderful?

HONORA. Wonderful. (*Pauses.*) Your Majesty, may I mention one thing more.

PRINCESS ALICIA. Anything. Anything.

HONORA. I just noticed something.

PRINCESS ALICIA. What is it? Tell me.

HONORA. You're smiling. And you are BEAUTIFUL.

PRINCESS ALICIA. Oh, Honora! (*Laughs heartily.*) Come. We have lots of work to do. (*They exit happily.*)

ACT II

SCENE. *The same garden three days later, Saturday, the twenty-first. On a large table, center stage, there are piles of clothing. As the scene opens, all the court ladies, and other women are busy sewing, consulting with* Honora's *mother, showing garments to* Honora, *and placing them on the piles.*)

MAIDEN. A few stitches more, and this will be finished.

PRINCESS ALICIA. Wonderful! Who would dream that you could sew like this?

ANOTHER MAIDEN. Look at this, Princess Alicia.

(King *and* Queen *enter left followed by knights and male workers.*)

KING. My gracious! You do have a pile of clothing! (*He walks around the table, looking at garments, followed by other newcomers except* Queen *who looks at clothing from where she is standing.*)

QUEEN. Daughter, I am so proud of you!

PRINCESS ALICIA (*happily*). Proud of me? Proud of all the women who have made clothing for Stillhope. (King *has taken his stand left, front.* Queen *is next to him.* Princess Alicia *about center stage.* Page *enters.*)

PAGE (*in formal manner*). May I announce— (King *nods.*) Prince Christoffo, heir apparent to the kingdom of Mountavalia! (Prince *enters. Bows to* King, Queen, *and* Princess Alicia.) And his cousin, Nathanial. (Nathanial *enters and bows.*)

KING. Prince Christoffo and Cousin Nathanial, I am delighted that you have come in person. Here are the garments that our women have made for the unfortunate people of Stillhope, in your kingdom of Mountavalia.

PRINCE (*looking right and left*). Thank you! Thank you! (*Walks to table. Picks up a garment.*) And such suitable clothing. Just what my people need. (*Bowing to* Queen.) Madam, on behalf of the people of Mountavalia, I thank you.

QUEEN. Pray, don't thank me. Thank my daughter, Princess Alicia. She directed the activity.

ALICIA. Don't thank me. Thank Honora. She told me of the need.

HONORA. Don't thank me. Thank my mother, who told us how to make suitable garments.

MOTHER OF HONORA. Don't thank me. Thank all the wonderful women who did the work.

PRINCE. I do thank you. Thank you, one and all. But how can I thank you? There must be some way. (*Pauses, thinking.*)

COUSIN NATHANIAL. I know, Cousin. Let's invite everyone to come to Stillhope. Let the people themselves say "Thank you."

PRINCE. Excellent! You must summon them right away. Harness your horses. (*Everyone is very still and downcast.*) What is the matter?

QUEEN. Your Highness, this is Saturday, the twenty-first.

PRINCE. Yes, I know. What of that?

QUEEN. Undoubtedly you were too busy to notice the invitation that was sent to all Princes. This is the night of the annual ball.

PRINCE. And you are all going to the ball. How wonderful! (*All others shake their heads.*) What is the matter? Is there something you cannot mention?

PRINCESS ALICIA (*stepping forward*). I am not going to the ball.

PRINCE. You, the Princess Alicia, not going to the ball? Why not?

PRINCESS ALICIA (*smiling softly*). This is the Ball of the Beautiful Maidens, and I am not beautiful.

PRINCE. Not beautiful? Rubbish! (*Speaks slowly.*) When I first entered this garden and I saw you standing there smiling, I thought, "There is the most beautiful princess in all the world, a princess who smiles from her heart."

PRINCESS ALICIA. Oh, Your Highness!

PRINCE (*to* King). Sire, may I escort your daughter, Princess Alicia, to the Ball of the Beautiful Maidens?

KING. Of course. (Prince *offers arm to* Princess Alicia *as* King *continues.*) And Cousin Nathanial may escort Honora, Princess of the Grand Order.

OTHERS. Princess Honora?

KING. Yes, Princess Honora, the maiden who taught my daughter to smile from her heart.

(*Everyone expresses delight, as* Cousin Nathanial *offers his arm to* Honora. *Everyone takes a partner. Group forms a procession which follows* King *and* Queen *offstage as curtain falls.*)

PLAY A PART

O LITTLE TOWN

Introduction

As you read this play, ask yourself, "What were the general working conditions in the United States just after the Civil War? How could a widow with a family make a living when only the lowest paid jobs were open to women? How could children help to keep the family together?"

Finding the answers to these questions will help you understand why Mrs. Bailey, a widow, feels that she is lucky to be able to work in the New England Knitting Mills, twelve hours a day, six days a week. Many other widows at this time were forced to turn their children over to "Overseers of the Poor," who placed the children as "bound children." As a rule these children worked without pay for farmers or craftsmen, or worked as household servants until they were twenty-one years old. Bound children usually went to school only when they were not needed in the fields and shops. The farmer, shop keeper, or master of the household gave his "bound boy" sufficient food and clothing in return for his labor.

Because of these general conditions, everyone in the Bailey family knows that being able to keep the family together is an achievement. They know it is possible only because they all work together. This spirit of togetherness and the joy of helping each other must show through in every line that is spoken and in every action. The fact that the Baileys are able to establish a special fund and the fact that they even dare to dream of sending a girl away from home to study music sets them apart as a very special family.

In order to make the wealthy Mr. and Mrs. Tomkins and Mr. Carncross believable you must understand the thinking of this period. A strong feeling of "class" existed. Many rich people felt that they ought to help the poor, but all too few tried really to understand the poor and their problems. Mr. and Mrs. Tomkins think that they are being most benevolent when they offer to adopt one of the teen-aged Bailey children and, in effect, ask him to desert his family and live an entirely different kind of life than he has known. Somehow the Tomkinses and Mr. Carncross think, as did many other people of the time, that a rich life is the only good life. The conflict in the play comes when the Bailey children, young as they are, see that this is not necessarily true.

Reading poems written during this period and books such as those by Louisa M. Alcott will show you that people were inclined to express their emotions and to talk freely about such subjects as "hopes and fears" and "everlasting light." The challenge of the play comes in showing how first Mrs. Tomkins, and then Mr. Tomkins and Mr. Carncross discover that people without money can be rich in other ways, and how people who have money sometimes need help from the poor. In the play Mary is a cripple and must learn to use a crutch effectively. She is also a person who shows musical promise. She need not be a violinist. She could play any instrument, or even sing. She could easily be older than Susan or John. Or, she could be smaller than Tom.

Study the tempo of the play. Decide which lines are important because they give atmosphere and which lines advance the plot and lead to the climax. Atmosphere lines must be said quickly. The feeling of the scene counts more than the thought carried by individual words. For example, at the opening of the play the audience must see a family happily preparing for Christmas even though the father is dead and there is little money. This scene must not drag.

However, when the word "fund" is mentioned, the lines must come out strong and clear. The fund plays a big part in the plot.

In like manner, the lines used in greeting the visitors register pleasure and surprise. No one line is really important. Guests and family must be seated as soon as possible. During this period the audience gets an impression of the character of the two pompous business men, who are very pleased with themselves and each other, and also of the sweet demure wife, proud of her "station in life."

The play grows earnest when the offer of adoption is made. Everyone must take this situation seriously and lead up to the dramatic moment of Mrs. Tomkins' "revelation."

After you understand the background and spirit of the play, map out action for your particular stage. You may want to make certain changes. For example, if the stage is full size, you may want to add small chairs so that girls can be seated during the conversation with guests. If you do not have a central backstage door, you will have to change exits, and certain other stage actions.

Then produce the play about a situation that might have happened in a small town in 1869. Convince the audience that although conditions in the country have changed, the play has meaning today.

Characters

JOHN BAILEY, oldest of the Bailey children
SUSAN BAILEY, older girl
MARY BAILEY, crippled younger sister
TOM BAILEY, youngest of Bailey children
MRS. BAILEY, widow and knitting-mill worker
MR. CARNCROSS, owner of New England Knitting Mills, Inc.
MR. C. WESLEY TOMKINS, owner of Boston's finest emporium
MRS. SARAH TOMKINS, his wife
VILLAGE CAROLERS

SCENE. *The Bailey home in a small New England town on Christmas Eve, 1869. Furnishings are modest, well-worn but neat, giving a feeling that the family has once seen better days. A Christmas tree, decorated with handmade paper ornaments and strung with popcorn, stands upstage right. Furnishings include two chairs with a table between them downstage, left; a comfortable chair, downstage, right; a straight-back chair, just right of center and a little back; a music stand in a corner; and other suitable furnishings that won't crowd the stage. Old books, a bowl of holly or other greenery, and other old-fashioned articles make the room look homey. Door leading to the street is placed upstage, center. Exit to other part of house is at the left.*

The scene opens with a group of carolers and Bailey children singing "God Rest You Merry, Gentlemen."

SUSAN (*at end of song*). Thank you. Thank you. It was very nice of you to come!

FIRST CAROLER. Don't thank us. Thank your Pa, God rest his soul. It was he who taught us how to sing.

SECOND CAROLER. It wouldn't be Christmas Eve without a song at the Bailey home.

THIRD CAROLER. Sorry your Ma wasn't home.

JOHN. She'll be sorry, too.

FIRST CAROLER. Must be on our way.

(Carolers *exit center, saying* "Goodbye" *and* "Merry Christmas" *to the Bailey children.* John, *being the oldest, plays host at the door.* Mary, *using her crutch, crosses to tree.* Susan *stands behind a small table, gets out a box and a patchwork pillowcase.* Tom *goes downstage, right, and stands behind large chair. Pounds the back as if irritated before he speaks.*)

TOM. Why did Ma have to miss the carolers again?

SUSAN. You know why. Ma is still working at the mill, where she has worked six days a week, twelve hours a day, ever since Pa was killed in the war.

MARY. And Ma says she's lucky to have a job and keep the family together.

TOM. I know. But why does she have to work on Christmas Eve?

JOHN (*coming downstage and imitating pompous* Mr. Carncross). Because, my dear fellow, in the words of the eminent Mr. Carncross, owner of New England Knitting Mills, Incorporated, "Inasmuch as the benevolent management has seen fit to honor its employees with a full day of rest on Christmas Day, it behooves said employees to repay the benevolent management with a benevolent willingness to work extra hours on Christmas Eve and on the day after Christmas." Simple, isn't it? (*Others laugh.*)

SUSAN. Well, I think it's simply wonderful that Ma keeps Christmas fun, even without Pa.

MARY. She says it's because we work together. (*Others nod.*)

SUSAN. Just the same, I'm glad I have a gift for Ma on Christmas Day.

JOHN. Sue, you didn't?

SUSAN. Didn't what?

JOHN. You didn't touch the fund.

SUSAN. Gracious no! See. (*Holds up pillow made of patches.*) I used scraps that Mrs. Crosby gave me.

(*Others gasp and exclaim* "Beautiful" "Marvelous" *as* Susan *puts her gift under the tree.* John *exits, left, briefly.*)

MARY. I have a gift, too, all wrapped. (*Points to box under tree.*) It's a carrot suet pudding. A new recipe from Mrs. Bixby.

TOM. You aren't the only ones. I got something from the store.

OTHERS. Tom! You didn't?

TOM. Touch the fund? Noooo—I got scrap lumber from the store. Made this. (*Shows carved figure. Others remark* "lovely" *as* Tom *puts the figure in a small box he has in his pocket and places the gift under the tree.* Sue *returns to table, left, to put objects in order as* John *enters, left, with stool behind his back.*)

JOHN. Me, too. (*Produces stool and holds it up for all to admire.*) Found it in the loft. New dowels. Lots of sanding. I'll put it back of the tree. Too hard to wrap. (*Door is flung open.* Mrs. Bailey *enters.*)

MRS. BAILEY. Merry Christmas!

CHILDREN. Merry Christmas, Ma.

MRS. BAILEY (*looking around*). Beautiful! The greens, the tree, gifts—children, you didn't?

CHILDREN. No, Ma, we did not touch the fund.

MRS. BAILEY. Good. But I can't wait till Christmas morning. I have to give you something now. (*Goes to table.*)

CHILDREN. Ma, did you?

MRS. BAILEY. No, I did not touch the fund. But I have something just right for Christmas Eve. (*Takes sheet music from drawer.*)

CHILDREN. It's music.

MA. Yes, a new carol. A woman at the mill received it from a friend in Boston. She copied it for me to give to you. (*Children gather round as* Mrs. Bailey *sits downstage.*)

SUSAN. I can read it.

OTHERS. So can I.

MARY. I'll play it. (John *gets music stand as* Mary *gets violin.* Mary *plays a few lines of* "O Little Town of Bethlehem." *Others sing softly. Loud knocking at door interrupts the carol singing. All speak at once as* John *goes to the door.* Tom *puts stand in corner.* Mary *puts her violin down.*)

SUSAN. Who can that be?

MARY. On Christmas Eve?

MRS. BAILEY. Maybe the carolers.

TOM. No, they've been here.

JOHN (*opening door*). Mr. Carncross. Come in.

(MR. CARNCROSS *enters, followed by* Mr. *and* Mrs. Tomkins.)

MRS. BAILEY. Mr. Carncross, what an honor! On Christmas Eve!

MR. CARNCROSS. Thank you, and this is Mrs. Tomkins and Mr. Tomkins of Boston. Mr. and Mrs. Tomkins, Mrs. Bailey. (*Adults exchange greetings.*)

MRS. BAILEY. And these are my children, Susan, Mary, John, and Tom. (Tom *and* John *shake hands with* Mr. Tomkins *as* Susan *and* Mary *bow slightly, saying,* "How do you do?")

(Mr. *and* Mrs. Tomkins *sit in chairs at the left;* Mr. Carncross *in the large comfortable chair.* Tom *brings the small chair, right, center downstage, with a space between this chair and* Mr. Tomkins. Tom *holds chair while* Mrs. Bailey *is seated.*)

MRS. TOMKINS (*adoringly*). So these are the children. (Baileys *are puzzled.*)

MR. CARNCROSS. Yes, these are the children.

MRS. BAILEY. Mr. Carncross, I'm surprised and honored—

MR. CARNCROSS (*interrupting*). I know you must be surprised on Christmas Eve. However, it seems to be an appropriate time to make a gift. (*Family looks at each other in surprise.*)

MR. TOMKINS. We want to do something most benevolent at Christmastime.

MR. CARNCROSS. I'll come to the point. Mr. Tomkins here—Mr. C. Wesley Tomkins—is president of The Emporium of Boston.

MR. TOMKINS. "Everything you want to buy under one roof."

MR. CARNCROSS. Largest retail store in the United States of America, and the best customer of New England Mills, Incorporated.

MR. TOMKINS. Producers of the finest woven materials in the world. (*They exchange pleased nods.*)

MR. CARNCROSS. Now to state our proposition bluntly. Mr. and Mrs. Tomkins have one sorrow.

MRS. TOMKINS. We are childless. (*Sniffs in her handkerchief.*)

MR. CARNCROSS. I have told Mr. and Mrs. Tomkins about this family; about the father who died in the War Between the States.

MRS. TOMKINS. God rest his soul.

MR. CARNCROSS. And about your noble struggle to keep alive in this little town.

MRS. BAILEY. Mr. Carncross, we love this little town. My late husband—

MR. CARNCROSS. Excuse me, Mrs. Bailey. The hour grows late, and it is Christmas Eve.

MRS. TOMKINS. And we've something wonderful to offer you.

MR. TOMKINS. My dear, let me tell them. (*Speaks pompously.*) Now, I have decided, or rather, my good wife and I have decided—that is, after learning of your wonderful qualifications, we have decided to adopt one of your children, Mrs. Bailey. (Baileys *are dumbfounded.*) That's what I mean. Actually adopt one of your children. I'll give him my name. I'll make him heir to my business.

MRS. TOMKINS. Rear him in Boston, not in this little town.

MRS. BAILEY. You mean adopt a full-grown child, not a baby?

MR. TOMKINS. Yes, Mrs. Bailey. It is done in Japan, my merchants tell me. Why adopt a baby with an unknown potential? Adopt a full-grown boy who is bound to succeed.

MR. CARNCROSS. Enough talk. Line up, children, so Mr. and Mrs. Carncross can judge for themselves which child they would like to adopt. (*Children look at* Mrs. Bailey, *who indicates that they should line up.*)

MR. TOMKINS (*rising and pointing to* John). Step forward, lad. (John *does so.*) You are John.

JOHN. Yes, sir.

MR. TOMKINS. John Tomkins. The name has a ring, don't you think?

JOHN. Sir, I am John Bailey, named after my late father. My place is here, in this little town. My mother, a widow, needs me to tend the garden, take care of repairs in the house, and do other chores while she works twelve hours a day at the mill. Sometimes I raise money for the fund.

MR. TOMKINS. But your future? Think of your future. Oh, you could visit your family once or twice a year, but your future would lie in Boston.

JOHN. My future, sir, lies in this little town. I plan to read law with Judge Hodges when I have finished public school.

MRS. TOMKINS. Wesley, how about the younger boy?

MR. TOMKINS. Well, that might not be so bad. I could mold him. Step forward, lad. (Tom *steps forward.*) Tell me, how would you like to become Thomas Tomkins?

TOM. I am sorry, sir. I am Thomas Bailey. My mother needs me, too. She'll need me more when John studies law. (*Speaks excitedly.*) And I give to the fund, too. I work at Anderson's grocery store. When I'm bigger, Mr. Anderson is going to open another store. He's going to make me manager, and—

MR. TOMKINS. Enough! Who wants an ungrateful son?

MRS. TOMKINS. Maybe a daughter.

MR. TOMKINS. Well, if it would please you. (*Addresses* Susan.) Step forward.

MRS. TOMKINS. Susan, would you like to come to Boston and be a fine lady, live in a big house, have servants, marry a rich young man?

SUSAN. Thank you, Mrs. Tomkins. I know you mean well, but my place is here, helping Ma. I, too, add to the fund. I make buttonholes for Mrs. Crosby the dressmaker.

MRS. TOMKINS. You each have spoken of the fund. What is the fund?

MR. CARNCROSS. Is something secret going on at the mill? Maybe I should spend more time in the mill.

MRS. BAILEY. No, no, Mr. Carncross, rest your mind. This is a family fund for my daughter Mary.

MR. CARNCROSS. The cripple.

MR. TOMKINS. It's noble to help a cripple.

JOHN, SUSAN, TOM. A cripple?

MR. CARNCROSS. Well, isn't Mary a cripple?

MRS. BAILEY. I'm sorry, sir. We tend to forget that Mary limps. We think only of her musical ability.

JOHN. Mary plays the violin very well. We want her to have a musical education.

MR. TOMKINS. Education for a girl? Whoever heard—

MARY. Excuse me, sir. I want a special kind of musical education. I want to teach music.

MRS. TOMKINS (*very interested*). Teach music?

MARY. Yes, teach music in this little town, just as my father did. Pa taught in his spare time, and I want to—

MR. TOMKINS. My dear young lady, are the people in this town sophisticated enough to appreciate a trained musician?

MARY. Sir, I want to teach simple music. Music that lifts the soul. Music like the carol Ma brought home tonight.

(Mr. Carncross *and* Mr. Tomkins *begin to fidget, look at watches, and so on, but* Mrs. Tomkins *shows increasing interest.*)

MRS. TOMKINS. What is the carol, Mary? Will you play it for me?

MARY. Gladly. (Mary *gets her violin while* John *sets up the music stand, center front. During this business* Mr. Carncross *and* Mr. Tomkins *carry on a little patter.*)

MR. TOMKINS. My dear, it is getting late.

MR. CARNCROSS. Very late.

MR. TOMKINS. We hate to keep people waiting.

MRS. TOMKINS (*firmly*). Please, Wesley. It is Christmas Eve. I want to hear the carol. We are ready, Mary.

(Mary *plays,* "O Little Town of Bethlehem" *as family hums, or if they are musicians, sing along softly. As* Mary *reaches the last line* Mrs. Tomkins *rises and walks front stage, facing audience. She is breathing heavily, as if struck with emotion or in a trance.*)

MRS. TOMKINS (*gasping*). Oh, oh—

(Mary *lowers her violin and stares.* Mr. Tomkins *goes quickly to his wife and puts his arm around her shoulder.*)

MR. TOMKINS (*with deep concern*). Sarah! Sarah, are you ill?

MR. CARNCROSS (*rising angrily*). Do something! Do something! Call the servants. You have no servants. Do something!

MRS. BAILEY (*going to* Mrs. Tomkins). Are you ill? May I help you? (Mary *puts her violin on the table.* Tom *removes music stand. Children come downstage.*)

MRS. TOMKINS (*regaining composure*). No, no. I'm sorry. It's the carol, the beautiful carol. I heard it first, last year.

MR. TOMKINS. Yes, my dear, in Trinity Church. It was written by the Rev. Phillips Brooks.

MRS. TOMKINS. Suddenly I remembered the words. "The hopes and fears of all the years." (*Everyone else relaxes.*)

MR. TOMKINS. A pleasant Christmas carol.

MR. CARNCROSS. A pretty tune.

MRS. CARNCROSS. You don't understand, Wesley. You just don't understand. (*All grow serious.*) You and I came here tonight, to this humble home in this little town, a town like Bethlehem. We were proud and haughty, because we thought we were wealthy. We wanted to do something for poor, downtrodden people.

MR. CARNCROSS. The ungrateful wretches.

MR. TOMKINS. I understand your disappointment.

MRS. TOMKINS. No disappointment, Wesley. Revelation.

(*Everyone is puzzled.*)

MR. TOMKINS. Revelation?

MRS. TOMKINS (*excitedly and happily*). We came here as proud, haughty, and wealthy people, pretending to do something for these poor, unfortunate people.

MR. TOMKINS. Well, we did want to—

MRS. TOMKINS. And we have found that they are not poor. They have a spirit we do not have. They are not unfortunate or downtrodden. They understand "the hopes and fears of all the years."

MR. TOMKINS. Well, I—

MRS. TOMKINS. Wesley, can't you see? In our brittle city life

we have no real understanding of the "everlasting light"?

Mr. Tomkins. Please, Sarah—

Mrs. Tomkins. Wesley, may I ask these people to help us? Please, on Christmas Eve!

Mr. Tomkins. Certainly. Anything to make you happy.

Mrs. Tomkins. Mary, come here, child. (Mary *hobbles forward on her crutch.*) Mary, when you go to study in Boston, where will you live?

Mary. I don't know, mam.

John. That's part of the problem.

Mrs. Bailey. John means that we have enough money for

Mary's lessons. We must provide funds for suitable lodging.

Mrs. Tomkins. Mary, would our home be "suitable"?

Mary. I can't leave my family.

Mrs. Tomkins. I don't mean that. I mean, will you live in our home while you attend school? (Mary *hesitates.*) Mary, you must study as soon as possible—first during the summers, and then full time. You must come back to this little town and teach music, just as your father did.

Mary. I hate to be beholden.

Mrs. Tomkins. Mary, try to understand. I don't want to give you anything. I want you to give us something. I am begging you, humbly begging you. Please live with us a little while. Fill our home with hope. Show us the meaning of "the everlasting light."

MR. TOMKINS. Please, Mary. (Mary *turns to others as if questioning.*)

OTHER CHILDREN AND MRS. BAILEY (*joyfully*). Yes, Mary, yes!

MR. CARNCROSS. Go ahead, Mary. Tell her you will.

MARY (*dropping her crutch and bowing low*). Thank you, mam.

MRS. TOMKINS (*helping her rise*). No, Mary, let me thank you.

MR. TOMKINS. Yes, thank you, Mary. And Merry Christmas to you all. In fact I'd like to say—(*He stretches his arms wide.*) Merry Christmas to everyone in this blessed little town.

(*A recording of* "O Little Town of Bethlehem" *is played offstage as the curtain closes on the scene of all the other characters responding with* "Merry Christmas to You!"

THERE'S ALWAYS A LEADER

Introduction

In order to portray the characters in this play, you must first understand some of the ideas people held at this time. Before you begin to study and memorize lines, read the background information which the narrator will give the audience. (See narrator's speech, page 221.) When you are familiar with the background, then consider the following points about the people in the play.

Captain Grey, in his role of factor or manager of the trading post, Fort Hall, is a loyal employee of the Hudson's Bay Company. Gentlemanly and efficient, he is dedicated to the proposition that Americans should not settle in Oregon in great numbers. He has convinced himself also that he is helping American pioneers by persuading them to go to California rather than to Oregon. Everything he says about the route to Oregon is true.

Caleb Greenway is not at all like Captain Grey. Greenway is slick, talkative, and a dandy, even in the wilderness. He seems to know everything. He never states his position or tells why he wants the pioneers to go to California. We may assume that he may be a land promoter in California, or a secret agent of the Hudson's Bay Company, or just a busybody. Certainly he is not an honest, forthright man. He does not mind stretching a point. The way to California was never "real easy."

Because these two men are different in personality, they must speak differently and act differently. The contrast must be very evident in the first scene. As you study these two characters, decide which of their lines best help the audience understand the purpose of the play and the historical background. Emphasize those lines, saying them slowly and directly to the audience. In the first scene Captain Grey states the theme of the play, "There's always a leader—as stubborn as the land he hopes to tame. He leads the others on to Oregon." This line requires perfect timing.

Decide which lines are only fill-in or background. Say these lines quickly as men shake hands, look around, cross the stage, sit down, and so on. Use stage business to perfect your timing and to convey a mood. Stage business is, of course, those little casual movements or actions, such as getting out a pipe, or tapping an envelope, or brushing imaginary lint from a shoulder. Use enough stage business to give the impression that this is a natural meeting of frontier people and not a series of speeches; but do not allow these bits of action to detract from the purpose of the play.

As the play progresses, be sure to continue to sharpen the individual characterizations which have been established for Captain Grey and Caleb Greenway. As the two men meet and greet the pioneers and talk with them, it must always be obvious that Captain Grey is honest in his remarks and that Greenway is underhanded and sly.

Jonathan is an idealistic teen-ager, forced to assume the role of a man. Like his father now dead, Jonathan is filled with the ideal of making Oregon a part of the United States. He is polite to his elders, but as the play progresses he feels increasingly that he is being pushed into doing something not consistent with his ideal. He stands his ground firmly, getting more and more resolute with each speech. Practice these speeches out loud until you make your voice build up to the climax.

All of the pioneers are hot, weary, and more or less at wits' end, wondering what they should do. Evans, a fatherly type and more or less leader of the group without a guide, is willing to listen and weigh information. Kelly and Mrs. Coates are the "action now" type, easily swayed by any self-appointed authorities. Each pioneer in the play must decide just how to express his weariness, concern, and interest in the decision-making conversation. He must decide at what points stage business, such as wiping his brow or smoothing the hair of a child, will add atmosphere. He must decide also when to pay undivided attention to what is being said and how to react. He must be a weary but interested pioneer every moment he is onstage. The enthusiasm of the group of pioneers brings the play to its climax.

Joe Meek is a historic character. If you want to portray him in depth, study a biography of him or read about him in other books about the trappers and early settlers in Oregon. In his youth Meek was a mountain man with a strange mixture of toughness and politeness. In his later years he became a leading citizen of Oregon. In 1848 he and nine companions crossed the Rockies and proceeded to Washington, D.C., to plead the cause of admitting Oregon as a territory of the United States.

In this play Meek follows a pattern of behavior that he developed as a mountain man. He bides his time and stays in the background listening and watching. At exactly the right moment he steps forward and says what he has to say clearly and effectively.

Characters

Narrators (two)
Captain Grey, factor at Fort Hall
Caleb Greenway, visitor
Jonathan Buckley, teen-age pioneer
Becky Buckley, his sister
Timothy Buckley, his brother
Mr. Evans, Mrs. Coates, Mr. Kelly — Pioneers
Other pioneers
Stranger

Scene. *Outside Fort Hall near the juncture of the Snake and Portneuf Rivers, about 1842. A background painting of Fort Hall with its white adobe walls would add to the atmosphere of the play. A red flag with the initials H. B. C. proclaims this to be the property of the Hudson's Bay Company. The fort should have a usable door. Two crude benches are placed downstage, left.*

First Narrator (*stands in front of curtain*). When our country was very young, a number of Americans were opposed to any annexation of western lands. Many agreed with Daniel Webster who said, "To what use could we ever hope to put those great deserts, or those endless mountain ranges, impenetrable, and covered to their bases with snow? What use have we for such a country? Mr. President, I will never vote one cent from the public treasury to place the Pacific coast one inch nearer to Boston than it is now."

SECOND NARRATOR. Other people feared it would be impossible to protect a territory so far from Washington, D.C. There were some who hoped Oregon and other western lands would become an independent country, friendly to the United States. Thomas Jefferson said, "I look forward with gratification to the time when descendants of the settlers of Oregon would spread themselves through the whole length of the coast, covering it with free, independent Americans, unconnected with us but by ties of blood and interest, and enjoying like us the rights of self-government."

FIRST NARRATOR. However, a large number of Americans believed in what they called "manifest destiny." They believed it was God's will that Oregon be an American territory. They believed it their God-given duty to settle Oregon, establish a government there, and work toward union with the United States.

SECOND NARRATOR. Officials and employees of the powerful, British-owned Hudson's Bay Company, and many French Canadians living in Oregon, hoped that Oregon would remain sparsely settled and eventually come under British rule. If this were not possible, then they felt the best alternative was to have Oregon become an independent country. The Hudson's Bay Company followed a very definite policy of trying to dissuade Americans from settling in Oregon.

FIRST NARRATOR. The scene of our play is just outside Fort Hall, a Hudson's Bay trading post where the Snake River joins the Portneuf River. The year is 1842.

(*As the play opens,* Captain Grey *emerges from the fort, breathing deeply, straightening his shoulders and rubbing his eyes as one would do after working on account books for some time.* Grey *comes downstage center, as* Greenway *enters right.*)

GREENWAY. Hello, hello!

CAPTAIN GREY. Hello, sir, and welcome to Fort Hall, trading post of the Hudson's Bay Company.

GREENWAY (*looking around*). Indeed! Indeed! The one and only Hudson's Bay Company, chartered in England, and subject to the orders of her majesty's government. Let me introduce myself—I am Caleb Greenway, newly come from California.

CAPTAIN GREY (*extending his hand*). How do you do, Mr. Greenway. I am Captain Grey, factor of Fort Hall. (*They shake hands.*)

GREENWAY. How do you do? I understand you haven't been here long?

CAPTAIN GREY. Not very long. Would you like to see the fort or (*motioning to benches*) rest a bit after your trip?

GREENWAY. Sit down, I think. 'Twould go good to sit down and chat, if I am not interrupting you.

CAPTAIN GREY (*going to bench farthest left*). You're not interrupting. Fresh air seems good after working on the books all morning.

GREENWAY. Doing a lively business, are you?

CAPTAIN GREY (*crossing legs in a relaxed manner*). Lively enough. Flour, twenty dollars a hundred. Horses, fifteen to twenty-five dollars a head. Shipped out a few pelts—

GREENWAY. I understand the fur trade is not what it used to be.

CAPTAIN GREY. No, trapping's not what it used to be. Some mountain men now are guides. Some are farmers.

GREENWAY. I understand your trade is with wagon folks, people passing through. Oh, I almost forgot. (*Takes letter from pocket.*) Letter for you. Looks as if it came from the home office. (*Hands letter to* Captain Grey, *who opens it.*) Captain of a ship heard I was coming this way.

CAPTAIN GREY. Mind if I look at the letter?

GREENWAY. Not at all. Go right ahead. (*He looks slowly around at the fort, appearing not to miss a single detail.*) Wagon folks are lucky to have Fort Hall. Gives them a chance to rest up before going on. Say, where are folks going these days? Oregon or California?

CAPTAIN GREY (*looking up from his letter*). I beg your pardon?

GREENWAY. I say "Where are folks going these days? Oregon or California?"

CAPTAIN GREY. Oregon mostly, if they're Americans. And most of them are Americans. That's the problem.

GREENWAY. Problem, indeed. If enough Americans go to Oregon, Oregon will become a part of the United States.

CAPTAIN GREY. Now, the Hudson's Bay Company being British—(*Pauses as if he doesn't want to say what he is thinking.*)

GREENWAY. I understand exactly what you mean. The Hudson's Bay Company, being an English company, would like to see the Americans go to California, leaving Oregon for the British. Fort Hall is the spot where men decide—California or Oregon? So it's up to you to persuade men to go to California. Simple, isn't it?

CAPTAIN GREY. Simple? Well, maybe it is simple for a man sitting in London at the home office. Here it is in black and white, just as if you had seen this letter. (*Reads from letter.*) "Please be advised: Encourage as many American settlers as possible to change route and go to California. For the best interests of the Hudson's Bay Company, Oregon must either become an independent country or become officially British. It must not become American . . ." and so on, and so on— (*Folds letter.*)

GREENWAY. I understand. And so on, and so on.

CAPTAIN GREY (*holding up folded letter*). Did you ever try to persuade an American to go to California when he was determined to go to Oregon?

(Greenway *shrugs as if he understands.*)

CAPTAIN GREY. You may persuade a few. But there's always a leader, as stubborn as the land he hopes to tame. He leads the others on. (*Sounds offstage indicate group is arriving at Fort Hall.*)

JONATHAN (*offstage*). Steady, boy!

MRS. COATES (*offstage*). Is this Fort Hall?

EVANS (*offstage*). Indeed it is, mam.

CAPTAIN GREY. Here comes another group. (*Stands. Puts letter in his pocket. Straightens his clothing and throws back his shoulders as* Greenway *goes right and seems to look at approaching group.*)

GREENWAY (*turning to* Captain Grey). Americans, all right. (*Crosses to* Captain Grey.) Sorry-looking sight.

CAPTAIN GREY. You'd be sorry-looking, too, if you'd walked as far as they have.

GREENWAY. Well, I'll let you greet them. (*Goes upstage as pioneers enter, right.*)

CAPTAIN GREY (*standing erect, center front stage*). Ladies and gentlemen, welcome to Fort Hall.

EVANS (*stepping forward and extending hand*). Evans is my name.

CAPTAIN GREY (*shaking hands*). I am Captain Grey, factor of Fort Hall. Can I be of service to you?

EVANS. Indeed you can, sir. Oh, this is Mr. Coates, Mr. Kelly (*introduces each man in turn*), and their womenfolk and children. (*Everyone exchanges greetings of* "Howdy," "How'd y' do," "Pleased to meet you," *and so on. Some remain right and others cross over, left.* Mrs. Coates *sits on bench farthest left, and* Mr. Kelly *on the other bench. All are hot and tired. Some of the women sit on the ground, as children nestle heads in their laps.*)

CAPTAIN GREY. And who is this young man? Your son?

EVANS. No, no, wish he were. This is Jonathan Buckley. His Ma and Pa died along the way. The boy lost his riggin', all but one cow. But he kept his cow and his brother and sister marching until they caught up with us.

CAPTAIN GREY (*extending hand*). Glad to meet you, Buckley. Or is it Jonathan? More like man than boy you are.

JONATHAN (*shaking hands*). Thank you, sir.

CAPTAIN GREY (*to all people*). Make yourselves at home, folks. Sit, or stand where you can. When you are rested, we'll bargain for supplies.

EVANS. Well, sir, what we want first is information.

CAPTAIN GREY. Information?

EVANS. Yes, information about the route to Oregon. We are traveling without a guide. (Stranger *enters left unnoticed.* Greenway *steps forward quickly.*)

GREENWAY. Oh, now are you set on Oregon?

EVANS. Well yes, sir, we are set for Oregon.

CAPTAIN GREY. Excuse me, sirs. This is Caleb Greenway, newly come from California.

EVANS. California? Mexican, isn't it?

GREENWAY. Mexican now. American, someday maybe. Who knows?

JONATHAN. Oregon will be American someday. That's what my Pa said. If enough Americans settle in Oregon, Oregon will become a part of the United States of America. Pa wanted to help make Oregon an American territory. I aim to carry out his wish by farming there.

GREENWAY (*getting out his unlit pipe and speaking slowly*). Well,. Oregon is all right for those who like to tell hard tales.

KELLY. What do you mean?

GREENWAY. You tell him, Captain Grey.

CAPTAIN GREY. Well, sir, from all reports, going to Oregon is mighty grim business.

JONATHAN. But people do get through. We heard so! (*Emphatically but as if reassuring himself.*)

CAPTAIN GREY. Oh, yes, some do get through, but many die of starvation and thirst on the way.

GREENWAY. Now, sir, the way to California is real easy. Ask me; I know. I just came back from there. Back and forth I go, real easy. (*He pauses as if a great idea just came to him.*) Of course, I'll not have much to talk about in my old age, like almost starving, and thirsting all the way to Oregon. I know about California. (*Points to* Jonathan.) What do you know about Oregon?

JONATHAN (*standing very straight*). I know a lot about Oregon. Joe Meek told my Pa, and my Pa told me.

GREENWAY. Do you know this Joe Meek?

JONATHAN. Well no, sir, never met him. But Joe Meek told my Pa how to get this far. And Joe Meek told my Pa how to get to the Willamette River in Oregon. That's where I plan to farm, right on the banks of the Willamette River.

KELLY (*standing*). So that's how you knew the way this far—secondhand from old Joe Meek.

CAPTAIN GREY (*putting arm around* Jonathan's *shoulder*). Now look, son. Did Joe Meek tell your father that you'll have to cross the Snake River twice?

JONATHAN. That's right. Twice. But I know I can—

CAPTAIN GREY. The Snake's no easy river. It's full of chutes, and rocks, and muddy water, running fast.

JONATHAN. I know. Joe Meek told my father. (Captain Grey *drops his arm and looks at* Greenway *as if to say*, "I told you so. There's always a leader." Greenway *steps up quickly and puts his arm around* Jonathan's *other shoulder.*)

GREENWAY. You really think you'll get to Oregon, boy? As I said before, going to California is real easy.

JONATHAN. Well, I aim to try my best.

MRS. COATES. What could we expect in California, Mr. Greenway?

GREENWAY. A right good life, mam, and weather so balmy it's no weather at all.

CAPTAIN GREY. In Oregon it rains all the time.

JONATHAN. Joe Meek told my father that Oregon has good soil and enough rain. With good workers, that means good crops.

CAPTAIN GREY. Who will buy your crops?

JONATHAN. Uh, I hadn't thought that far ahead, sir. Have to get there first.

GREENWAY. California has good markets.

JONATHAN. But California's Mexican—we aim to make Oregon part of the U.S.A.

GREENWAY (*speaking past* Jonathan *and to* Other Pioneers).

Don't let a boy persuade you. California has everything, except enough good workers. California needs good workers.

JONATHAN. Oregon needs good workers, too. Oregon needs American men and women. And the United States needs Oregon.

CAPTAIN GREY (*to large group*). Think it over. You may never reach Oregon. A few may get there, but not the lot of you. You'll have rivers to ford, mountains to climb, Indians to worry about. Snow's coming soon. And rain. And fevers. And snake-bites! Why should you go to Oregon? Why not go to California?

KELLY. Think on it: why should we be so set on going to Oregon? (*Most of the pioneers pantomime asking each other the same question.*)

MRS. COATES. We've no guide except the boy.

KELLY. And he got his information secondhand from Old Joe Meek. As for me, I'm going to California.

GREENWAY. All those going to California, step over here with me. (*He goes downstage right. Most of the pioneers gather around him. Others wait uncertainly.* Evans *goes to speak to* Jonathan, *who has remained at center stage.*)

EVANS. Where're you going, boy?

JONATHAN (*looking with disappointment at all those in the California group*). I—I have to go to Oregon. That's what my Ma and Pa set out to do. It's what I want to do—what I have to do.

GREENWAY. You could be sensible and go to California. You're responsible for that brother and sister and for getting them a home. (Other Pioneers *add a* "Yes" *or* "That's right.")

(Becky *and* Timothy *have come to stand beside* Jonathan.)

BECKY. What about those rivers, Jon? And the heavy snow?

TIMOTHY. Aw, Beck, Jonathan can manage, can't you?

JONATHAN (*straightening his shoulders*). We've got to go on. Ma and Pa—

CAPTAIN GREY (*addressing* Stranger *who has come slowly down-stage*). Well, stranger, where are you going?

STRANGER. I'm going with the young 'uns to Oregon. (*He steps deliberately to the left to stand beside* Jonathan, Becky, *and* Timothy.) And we'll get to Oregon just like his old Pa said.

KELLY. Fool! (*He shouts in disbelief.*) Trusting a kid for a guide.

GREENWAY. What makes you think you can get to Oregon, old man?

STRANGER. The young 'uns and me—we'll make it!

CAPTAIN GREY. Who are you, anyway?

STRANGER. My name's Meek.

CAPTAIN GREY. Joe Meek? The famous mountain man?

KELLY. Joe Meek, the guide?

STRANGER. Yep. Old Joe Meek, you called me awhile back. (*He turns to look squarely at* Jonathan.) I'm Joe Meek, a farmer, now, and a citizen of Oregon. (*He extends his hand to* Jonathan.)

OTHERS. Joe Meek. It's really Joe Meek!

STRANGER (MEEK). I'm glad to meet you Jonathan. Your Pa was right, of course. Oregon needs folks like you, and the United States needs Oregon—

EVANS (*interrupting*). I really wanted to go to Oregon. (*He steps to* Jonathan's *side.*)

KELLY, MRS. COATES, AND OTHERS. Me, too! Me, too!

CAPTAIN GREY (*as* Greenway *slinks offstage*). Jonathan, I meant every word I said. It is rough, wild country, but there's always a leader as stubborn as the land. This time the leader was a young man, scarcely more than a boy, a boy named Jonathan.

JONATHAN. And a guide named Joe Meek.

EVANS. Will you guide us, Joe? Guide us all to Oregon?

MEEK. You bet. I'll guide you all to Oregon.

JONATHAN. We'll make it. The United States needs Oregon—

ALL THE OTHER PIONEERS. AND OREGON NEEDS FOLKS LIKE US! (*Pioneers cheer as curtain is drawn.*)

FIRST NARRATOR. Oregon became the thirty-third state of the United States of America on February 14, 1859.

GLOSSARY OF A FEW STAGE TERMS

AD LIB To make up lines or add words on the spur of the moment.

BLOCK OUT A SCENE To plan position of players and their changes of position in a scene.

CLIMAX Highest point of dramatic tension in play.

CUE A speech or action in a play that serves as a signal for another actor to speak or act.

DEAD PAN No expression in face.

DIALOGUE Conversation in a play.

DOWNSTAGE The part of the stage nearest the audience.

KEY LINES Lines that must be emphasized if the audience is to follow the plot or understand the message or joke of a play.

LEFT STAGE The part of thc stage on the actors' left when they are facing the audience.

NARRATOR One who tells a story or describes for an audience the setting of a story and outlines the action or incidents that "have gone before."

OFFSTAGE Behind the scenes.

ONSTAGE The area which the audience sees.

PANTOMIME The art of acting silently, portraying a situation or an attitude with bodily movements and facial expression but no sound.

PLOT Story and action of a play.

PROPS Shortened term for "properties"; any moveable object necessary to the action of a play.

PUNCH LINE The line in a play that makes the point of the joke or message.

PUPPETEER One who manipulates or handles puppets in a show or other performance.

RIGHT STAGE The part of the stage on the actors' right when they are facing the audience.

SCRIPT The written or printed play.

SET, SETTING Arrangement of furniture and properties.

STAGE BUSINESS Actor's action intended to create atmosphere or reveal character—for example, nervous person lightly tapping tabletop with his fingertips.

UPSTAGE Part of the stage farthest from the audience.

WALK-ON A small part, usually without lines to speak.

OTHER BOOKS TO HELP YOU

Books for Boys and Girls

As your interest in dramatics grows, you may want to learn a great deal more about acting. You will want to be familiar with more plays. These books may help you:

Bendick, Jean, and Berk, Barbara. HOW TO HAVE A SHOW. New York: Franklin Watts, 1957.

Boy Scouts. BEAR CUB SCOUT BOOK. New Brunswick: Boy Scouts of America, 1967.

THEATER. Merit Badge Series. New Brunswick: Boy Scouts of America, 1968.

WEBELOS SCOUT BOOK. New Brunswick: Boy Scouts of America, 1967.

WOLF CUB SCOUT BOOK. New Brunswick: Boy Scouts of America, 1967.

Carlson, Bernice Wells. ACT IT OUT. Nashville: Abingdon Press, 1956.

DO IT YOURSELF. Nashville: Abingdon Press, 1952.
THE RIGHT PLAY FOR YOU. Nashville: Abingdon Press, 1960.
Fenner, Phyllis, and Hughes, Avah. ENTRANCES AND EXITS. New York: Dodd, Mead, 1960.
Girl Scouts. BROWNIE GIRL SCOUT HANDBOOK. New York: Girl Scouts of the United States of America, 1963.
JUNIOR GIRL SCOUT HANDBOOK. New York: Girl Scouts of the United States of America, 1963.
CADETTE GIRL SCOUT HANDBOOK. New York: Girl Scouts of the United States of America, 1963.
SENIOR GIRL SCOUT HANDBOOK. New York: Girl Scouts of the United States of America, 1963.
Howard, Vernon. SHORT PLAYS FROM THE GREAT CLASSICS. New York: Sterling Publishing Co., 1960.
Jagendorf, Moritz. PUPPETS FOR BEGINNERS. Boston: Plays, Inc., 1952.
Martin, Judith. LITTLE PLAYS FOR LITTLE PEOPLE. New York: Parents' Magazine Enterprises, Inc., 1965.
Severn, Bill and Severn, Sue. LET'S GIVE A SHOW. New York: Alfred A. Knopf, 1956.
Smith, Moyne R. PLAYS AND HOW TO PUT THEM ON. New York: Henry Z. Walck, 1961.
Thane, Adele. PLAYS FROM FAMOUS STORIES AND FAIRY TALES. New York: Alfred A. Knopf, 1952.
Tichenor, Tom. FOLK PLAYS FOR PUPPETS YOU CAN MAKE. Nashville: Abingdon Press, 1959.

Books for Adult Leaders

Boleslavsky, Richard. ACTING, THE FIRST SIX LESSONS. New York: Theater Arts Books, 1949.
Crossup, Richard. CHILDREN AND DRAMATICS. New York: Charles Scribner's Sons, 1960.
Miller, Helen. POINTERS ON PRODUCING THE SCHOOL PLAY. Boston: Plays, Inc., 1960.
Walker, Pamela P. SEVEN STEPS TO CREATIVE CHILDREN'S DRAMATICS. New York: Hill and Wang, 1957.
Ward, Winifred. STORIES TO DRAMATIZE. Cloverlot, Kentucky: Anchorage Press, 1952.

INDEX

PLAY A PART

INDEX